PRAISE FOR *THE FORGOTTEN BEATITUDE*

Bill Tuck has delivered another useful tool for the Preaching Pastor and Congregation. This collection of sermons goes a long way in helping Pastor and Parish understand the depth of Stewardship. He begins with the simplicity of a one sentence parable and from there unpacks some of the best understanding for 21st Century Christian generosity! This is certainly a needed response to perhaps the most challenging of topics!

Bo Prosser, Ed. D., *Coordinator of Organizational Relationships,*
Cooperative Baptist Fellowship, Decatur, GA

We have come, across the years, to expect scriptural, down-to-earth, and extremely useful books from the prolific pen of Dr. William Tuck. This book of sermons on stewardship will not disappoint. One of its most valuable contributions, in my opinion, is its veritable multitude of simple and effective illustrations. Pastors who spend some time with these sermons will inevitably be inspired to address their own congregations on the truly spiritual nature of giving.

John Killinger, Ph.D., Th.D.
former pastor of First Congregational Church, Los Angeles
former professor at Vanderbilt Divinity School
and author of many books including
The Ministry Life: 101 Tips for New Ministers and
Fundamentals of Preaching.

As a former professor of preaching as well as a successful pastor, Bill Tuck combines his skills in a masterful fashion in this book of splendid stewardship sermons. Each sermon reflects the needs of actual congregations, is based in a thorough study of Scripture, and demonstrates a holistic understanding of stewardship. Too many pastors neglect the need to deal with financial issues in the church. In these sermons we see the biblical mandate of Christian stewardship presented in a wholesome and enthusiastic fashion. The book is illustrated in a marvelous fashion; any time you can laugh while listening to a stewardship appeal you know there is something special here.

Thomas Graves, Ph.D.
President Emeritus
The Baptist Theological Seminary at Richmond

William Tuck confesses that preaching about stewardship is a challenge. Then he rolls up his sleeves to help you get the job done. In sharing his collection of effective sermons, he outlines seventeen expositions of the most familiar Scriptures for giving and generosity and fills in the color with copious illustrations. This is the next resource you need in the stewardship section of your sermon library.

J. Robert Moon, D.Min, MBA
Consultant for Pastoral Care in the Context of Wealth,
Author of *My Pastor, My Money, and Why We're Not Talking*

OTHER BOOKS BY WILLIAM POWELL TUCK

The Way for All Seasons:
Reflections on the Beatitudes for the 21st Century

Facing Grief and Death: Living with Dying

The Struggle for Meaning (editor)

Knowing God: Religious Knowledge in the Theology of John Baillie

Our Baptist Tradition

Ministry: An Ecumenical Challenge (editor)

Getting Past the Pain

A Glorious Vision

The Bible as Our Guide for Spiritual Growth (editor)

Authentic Evangelism

The Lord's Prayer Today

The Way for All Seasons

Through the Eyes of a Child

Christmas Is for the Young... Whatever Their Age

Love as a Way of Living

The Compelling Faces of Jesus

The Left Behind Fantasy

The Ten Commandments: Their Meaning Today

Facing Life's Ups and Downs

The Church in Today's World

The Church Under the Cross

Modern Shapers of Baptist Thought in America

The Journey to the Undiscovered Country: What's Beyond Death?

A Pastor Preaching: Toward a Theology of the Proclaimed Word

The Pulpit Ministry of the Pastors of River Road Church, Baptist
(editor)

The Last Words from the Cross

Overcoming Sermon Block: The Preacher's Workshop

Holidays, Holy Days and Special Days

A Revolutionary Gospel:
Salvation in the Theology of Walter Rauschenbusch

Star Thrower: A Pastor's Handbook

A Positive Word for Christian Lamenting: Funeral Homilies

THE FORGOTTEN BEATITUDE

WORSHIPING THROUGH STEWARDSHIP

WILLIAM POWELL TUCK

Energion Publications
Gonzalez, FL
2016

ISBN10: 1-63199-328-3
ISBN13: 978-1-63199-328-2
Library of Congress Control Number: 2016962604

Energion Publications
P. O. Box 841
Gonzalez, FL 32560

energion.com
pubs@energion.com

With appreciation
To
Ruben Swint
Who has helped many churches learn
the significance of Christian stewardship.

TABLE OF CONTENTS

FOREWORD

Bill Tuck has provided a valuable resource for preaching in his latest book, *The Forgotten Beatitude: Worshiping through Stewardship.* The themes of worship and stewardship are rightly united. We are reminded that all of life comes from God and belongs to God and that fullness of life is discovered in the blending of "receiving" and "giving."

This volume contains seventeen sermons Dr. Tuck has preached in various churches where he has served as pastor. He provides a solid theological foundation for Christian stewardship that goes far beyond trite lessons about "duty to support the church." Biblical stewardship takes seriously our relationship to the material world as well as our interrelationship with all people everywhere. We are indeed our brother's keeper. The sermon on environmental theology is a unique and welcome word. The sermons are a testimony to the sacredness of all life and our joyful response to God's grace. Stories from personal life, from others and from Scripture add richness and variety to the sermons.

Success in life is defined not as accumulation of material goods but as appropriate response to grace. What comes *to* us is intended to go *through* us. Clearly, yet kindly, Dr. Tuck calls us to a life of missional living.

The sermons are articulate, challenging, theologically sound, and humbling. They will serve well as rich devotional material or as inspiration for pastors and church members. Each sermon ends with a brief prayer that strokes the chords of memory and draws out of us authentic gratitude.

Lee McGlone, Ph.D.
Pastor Emeritus, First Baptist Church, Arkadelphia, Arkansas
and former editor of *The Minister's Manual*

PREFACE

Rolling up one's sleeves is a simple, practical act. It is a symbolic act as well, signifying on the part of the sleeve-roller a commitment to work, an absorption in getting the job done, and a forgetting about incidentals and inconveniences. Commitment and absorption are important ingredients of stewardship. The cuff line is one of the fine lines that divide what is stewardship and what is not. Sleeve-rolling, however, is just an empty gesture unless getting to work becomes the next step. Stewardship is one of the essential means the church utilizes to roll up its sleeves and engage in the ministry it is challenged to do.

Sometimes it is easy to talk about what we want the local church to be and do, but unless we are willing to support it with our financial stewardship, our talk is just meaningless motion. The local church budget indicates that the church members are rolling up their sleeves as they look to the future. The church's budget indicates something about its goals, plans, and hopes for its local and world-wide church's ministries. Some of the church's most vital ministries cannot be undertaken without financial support. Don't get caught in the mistaken notion that a church budget is unspiritual. All spiritual realities must be expressed in material ways. The church's budget is both a guide and a picture of the potential that the church has, if the church's members are willing to be effective Christian stewards. It is a ladder of opportunity, but only to the extent that each member rolls up his or her sleeves and does one's share. The future for the church, I still believe, is bright with possibilities in spite of its many naysayers, but it involves the willingness of every member to roll up one's sleeves and become a part of the vital supporters of their local church.

Our giving to our local church must be an expression of the deeper giving of ourselves. God wants what we are and what we have to be dedicated to spiritual ends. Unless our gifts are expressions of personal devotion, they are merely futile gestures. If our gifts of time, talents, and money are expressions of a personal devotion to Christ, they become a channel through which we grow in the likeness of the Lord we love. The Dead Sea is dead because it receives and does not give. This condition is deadly for a sea; it is more deadly to a human soul. He or she who refuses to give refuses to live. Living is giving, sharing, serving, and loving. "It is more blessed to give than to receive" (Acts 20: 35b), Jesus reminds us.

Stewardship is rolling up our sleeves and sharing in the work of Christ's Kingdom. I believe the pastor of the local church has to challenge one's congregation to let their cuff-line be an indication of their commitment for Christ to support the ministry and programs of their church for each year. The pastor needs to be bold to declare that the church needs their support. He or she should ask the church members to reflect on what their church has meant to them and what they would like to help it mean to others. Call them to reflect on the sacrifice Christ made to found his church. As a pastor, I have not hesitated to urge my congregation to give to support the ministries of the church as set forth in the annual budget. I challenged them to give out of their love and loyalty to Christ who compels them to give their lives to Him and serve him as Lord. The church's giving helps to make the dream of what the local church can be in its community come into reality. I strive to challenge them to give with a sense of love, commitment, expectancy, and, if possible, extravagantly.

I believe that every pastor has the challenge of preaching sermons on stewardship to his or her congregation. Here in this collection are sermons I have shared with various congregations where I have served as pastor or interim pastor. The sermons are presented here as they were delivered with only a few changes. I have left the local challenges, figures, statics, etc. to show the very personal nature of the sermons as they were actually delivered. In one of the congregations, St. Matthews Baptist Church in Louisville, Kentucky, a fire had destroyed the church's sanctuary and a large part of the educational plant. The congregation faced a multi-million dollar building endeavor as they met in "borrowed" facilities for several years. I often had to preach sermons that challenged them to give to the annual budget and to the Building Fund as well. In my sermons I tried to remind the congregation of how much their church needed their commitment. Perhaps, as pastors, we have not always emphasized that enough. Every member of a congregation needs to be reminded of how much their pledge of support is important. I also attempted to note that their faithful giving was essential for the ongoing ministry of the church. I appealed to them to let their pledge/commitment card be a reflection of their deep commitment to the Christ who loves us and has challenged us to serve Him. Our stewardship always has to be linked to our deeper commitment to Christ as Lord. I want to express again my appreciation to my friend and fellow minister, Rand Forder, for graciously taking time to proofread the manuscript. May God help us all to be faithful stewards in our ministry for Christ.

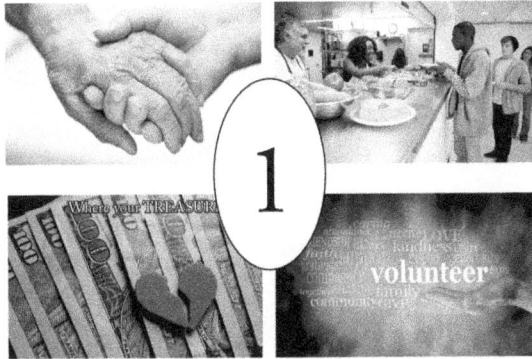

"THE FORGOTTEN BEATITUDE"

Acts 20:31-35

"It is more blessed to give than to receive." (Acts 20:35)

In his departing words to the Ephesian Christian leaders at the port of Miletus, the Apostle Paul cited one of the sayings of Jesus which has not been preserved in the Gospels. The only other place Paul quoted Jesus directly is found in 1 Corinthians 11:24-25 where he is describing the Lord's Supper. There are a number of places in his Epistles where he alluded to sayings of Jesus, but he did not quote them directly.[1] When Paul delivered his speech, the Gospels had not yet been written, but he was familiar with the sayings and teachings of Jesus which were passed on from one Christian group to another by word of mouth. Later, after writing his Gospel, John observed that there were so many other things which Jesus said and did, and if they were written down, the world could not contain all the books which would be written (John 21:25). The Gospels could not possibly include every word and deed of Jesus.

Paul's hearers were obviously familiar with this saying for he admonished them with the word *remember*. For them it was not an unknown Beatitude. He simply reminded them to fall back upon one of the sayings of Jesus which had been treasured up in

---

1   Some of these references may be found in Romans 14:14, 1 Corinthians 9:14; 1 Thessalonians 4:15f; Timothy 5:8.

the memory of the early disciples. Paul recounted this Beatitude with the assurance that it was known to the Christian community gathered before him. He entreated them to remember it on this occasion.

Paul's farewell speech poured forth like that of a pastor whose heart was filled with love and devotion for his people. He reminded them of his public ministry of teaching and his personal house-to-house visitation. His ministry had not been easy but was filled with trials and tears. Nevertheless, he had spoken fearlessly. He had supported himself by his own hands so he would not be dependent upon others and could give generously to them. He had exemplified by his life what he had taught. He told them that he would probably not see them again, but he felt compelled to go to Jerusalem to fulfill what he sensed the purpose of God was for him. He then charged them to be aware of the dangers within and without the church from those who wanted to destroy it. He warned them to preserve their own spiritual life and to nourish the people they were responsible for guiding.

Later, Ephesus and other churches in Asia Minor would experience the bloody persecution of Domitian and struggle with the heresies of the Nicolaitans and Gnosticism. When Paul finished speaking, he prayed for them and they embraced him and wept. Paul had labored longer in Ephesus than any other place, and he had grown to love these friends. In this brief passage we see Paul not as a great theologian, or a great preacher, but simply as a loving pastor.

In this tender moment Paul reached back in his memory of the teachings of Jesus to leave with them some saying that would guide them. They had no New Testament. The Gospels had not been written. Most of them probably could not read anyway. Suddenly Paul recalled the words. The use of double emphatic personal pronouns in the Greek text emphasized that Paul affirmed that these words were from Jesus. "Remember how *he himself* said, "It is more blessed to give than to receive." In this unforgettable sentence of Jesus, "It is more blessed to give than to receive," Paul presented a summary of the Lord's teachings. This golden saying casts its light upon the pathway for those who would follow Jesus, and it offers light and guidance for those who would travel in that direction.

It would be interesting to know the occasion of this Beatitude. Did Jesus utter it after the poor widow dropped in her mite at the Temple? Did He express it after the meal in the house of Zacchaeus when Zacchaeus stated that half of his goods he would give to the poor, and if he had defrauded anyone, he would restore fourfold? Did Jesus relay these words softly to His disciples as the rich young ruler walked away sorrowfully? Were they said with flashing eyes after the mother of James and John had tried to secure a special place in Christ's kingdom? Were they spoken tenderly after Jesus Himself had washed the disciples' feet? Were they voiced in anger to Simon after he had refused to wash the dust from Jesus' feet, and a woman had anointed them with ointment from an alabaster flask and then wiped them with her hair?

We do not know the setting. They may have been words said privately to His disciples or in a public sermon. Although we do not know the occasion, the sentence, "It is more blessed to give than to receive" still calls us back to the heart of the Christian faith. Unfortunately, we have reduced and hidden them only to be spoken before or after the offering in our worship services. But if we link these words only to our money, we may have missed the original thrust. This Beatitude summarizes Christian living, not just financial giving. It focuses on attitude, a way of life, a philosophy of living. *The New English Bible* translates the verse this way: "Happiness lies more in the giving than in receiving." This Beatitude points us toward the path that leads to real happiness.

THE BLESSING OF RECEIVING

"It is more blessed to give than to receive." The use of the phrase *more blessed* implies that there is a blessing in receiving. Our capacity to receive in a real sense determines our ability to give. If we do not understand the blessing of receiving, the higher blessing of giving will also elude us. Giving and receiving are not depicted as merely opposite sides of a coin. The comparison seems to suggest a difference between a higher and lower form of blessing. One is obviously greater and more important, but that does not indicate that the lesser has no value or significance. There is more blessedness in giving, but receiving carries with it a dimension of blessedness also. "Freely ye have received, freely give." (Matthew 10:8, KJV).

While I was in college and seminary, I had the privilege of serving as pastor of Good Hope Baptist Church, a rural church in northern Virginia. Although many years have passed since that time, I retain many delightful memories from my ministry there and have continued to stay in touch with that fine Christian community. One summer when we were having our annual church revival, the guest minister and I were visiting various members in the community. We had completed a nice visit with one of the poorer families in the community and walked to the front porch to leave. The lady of the house turned to me and said, "I have a bag of apples I would like to give you, Pastor."

I very graciously said, "Thanks. I appreciate that but I don't know how we could keep them right now."

As we got into the car to drive away, my friend Al said to me: "Bill, that was a mistake."

"What was?" I asked.

"When that lady offered you the apples," Al said, "you should have taken them. Although she was poor, she was still trying to share something with you out of her generous spirit and to show you some small appreciation for your ministry here."

He was right. In my youthful response I may have made the giver feel that her small gift was not worthy. Of course, I had not intended that. I was more concerned with where I could keep the apples later so they would not spoil. But I had missed the main point. Well, I have never forgotten that lesson and have tried to learn how to be a more gracious receiver through the years.

Most of us will have to admit, if we are really being honest, that we have difficulty in receiving. I always shuffle my feet and get tongue-tied if someone extends a compliment to me. Congratulations often leave me open-mouthed and feeling awkward. Upon receiving a gift, I often struggle with words that seem to communicate in only a clumsy way my real feelings of appreciation. Many of us receive with the lumbering grace of a hippopotamus. Our inability to accept praise often offends or rejects the person who is seeking to be gracious to us. This might really reflect more about our own insecurity and fears than we would like to admit even to ourselves.

Keith Miller related an experience which he had right after he had just given a talk in his church. A man, whom he respected very much, affirmed him enthusiastically with the compliment, "That was a great job, Keith!"

"Thanks, but I'm afraid I was too direct!" Miller replied. "I was tired and felt a little hostile." His friend looked at him strangely and then walked away into the educational wing of the church. In an instant, Miller knew what he had done. His friend had sincerely tried to express his appreciation. But instead of accepting his affirmation, Miller's actions told him that he was not really very smart because Miller picked up some negative things about the talk which his friend didn't hear. He realized that his negative response had in fact rejected his friend and the kindness which he had expressed through his praise. Miller, of course, had not meant to do that. "Never before had I realized fully the negative, squelching effect of refusing to accept another's kind words."[1]

A gift is indeed enriched or degraded by its reception. Anne Morrow Lindbergh wrote several years ago about an unforgettable character she knew named Edward Sheldon. "He knew how to receive so graciously," she said, "that the gift was enhanced by its reception. It was the rarest pleasure to bring things to him…warmed by his welcome, how beautiful became the things one brought to

---

1   Keith Miller, *Habitation of Dragons* (Waco, Tex.: Word Books, 1970), 88-89.

him."[1] Unfortunately, not many of us are like that. To receive graciously from someone who gives to us is, in reality, sharing a gift of our self with them. It is wrong merely to assume that the giver will know we are appreciative of the gift. We all know what a warm embrace, a sincere handshake, a thank-you note, or a phone call means to us when we have been the one who gave.

David Dunn was correct. There really is "a gracious art of receiving." He spoke about a niece of his that he felt had completely mastered the art of receiving compliments. "Giving her a compliment," he said, "is always an enjoyable experience." First, she gives a quick smile of appreciation, along with an equally quick "Thank you." This is then followed by a comment that takes the focus off herself. She might reply, for example by saying: "Yes, isn't it a pretty dress? Mother sent it to me." On another occasion she replied: "I got the idea for rearranging the room from so-and-so's new book on interior decorating." Her secret is clear. She has learned to accept the compliments only for a fleeting second and then passes them on to others.[2]

Many things are missed in life because we have not learned how to receive them. I might fill my house with books, but unless they are read they are not really received. I might walk through an art gallery filled with famous paintings, but without some sense of art appreciation I cannot receive what they offer. I may have hundreds of cassette tapes of classical music, but without some capacity to appreciate their quality I cannot receive them. I might enroll in a university and attend classes, but unless I am willing to receive knowledge which my teachers will impart, I cannot learn. Receiving is not easy. The best things are not acquired quickly or effortlessly. Before something is received into my life, I must have the capacity to welcome and admit its presence.

This means that I cannot remain neutral. Receiving is an act which requires response on my part. I do not really receive some-

---

1   Quoted in David Dunn, *Try Giving Yourself Away* (Englewood Cliffs, N.J.: Prentice-Hall, Inc., 1956), 84.

2   Ibid, 85.

thing if I am unwilling to accept it. Several years ago when I was travelling through the Bavarian mountains, I noticed that outside many of the houses the owners had placed large barrels to collect rainwater. The containers received the water so it might be used later. In a sense every life needs to be a container to receive. Without the act of reception, the gifts which are offered to me cannot be mine. Before the prodigal son could begin to receive, he had to return home. If he had remained in the far country, he would not have experienced his father's forgiveness.

One of the characters of the New Testament who struggled with his inability to receive was the rich young ruler. "Good Teacher, what must I do to inherit eternal life?" (Mark 10:17). Here within this young man were two forces at war. On the one hand, he thought he had to earn his eternal life. And on the other hand, he spoke of it as though it were a gift – an inheritance. Like too many today, the rich young ruler thought he had to earn or achieve his salvation. He had to give away something, not achieve something, and enter a life of service by following Him.

Salvation is a gift. At the very heart of the Christian faith is receiving. The gift of God is eternal life. It is a gift. The first Bible verse which most of us learn states, "For God so loved the world that he gave his only Son, that whoever believes in him should not perish but have eternal life" (John 3:16). Salvation is a gift. It is given by God. The root of most of the church's heresies has been the effort of men and women to earn their salvation rather than to receive it as God's loving gift. Remember the apostle Paul's ringing affirmation: "For by grace you have been saved through faith; and this is not your own doing, it is the gift of God - not because of works, lest any man should boast" (Ephesians 2:8-9).

So much of what we have in life comes to us as a gift. The world with its sunshine and rain, night and day, summer and winter, springtime and harvest, comes to us as a gift from the Creator. Our very life came to us as a gift from our parents. We had no design in it. The wealth under our feet in the earth's crust and the riches buried beneath the depths are gifts from the boundless provisions of nature. We are stewards of the earth, not its masters. We can appreciate the earth's bounty, discover it, utilize it, consume it, but first we must receive it.

In our churches, many of us are debtors to the people who, generations before us, gave sacrificially so we might worship in comfort today. We enjoy the benefits paid for by their foresight and willingness to give. When you sit in a church building which is over fifty years old, remember you are a receiver. You are a receiver of the thoughts, plans, efforts, and gifts of those who were here before you. None of us is independent. We are receivers all. We are receivers of electricity and telephones, heat and air-conditioning, automobiles and airplanes, radio and television, papers and books, houses and farms. We are the recipients of experiments, inventions, discoveries, explorations, and sacrifices of countless thousands through the course of history. We are debtors to them for their innumerable gifts, too countless to name. We stand on their shoulders of accomplishment and have received more than we ever could repay.

Years ago a wealthy student who was attending Williams College was accused of defacing some of the college property. When he came in to see the college president, Mark Hopkins, he arrogantly whipped out his checkbook and asked how much was it going to cost him to pay for the damages. President Hopkins ordered the young man to sit down and exclaimed: "No man can pay for what he receives here. Can you pay for the sacrifice of Colonel Williams who founded the college? Can you pay for the half-paid professors who have remained here to teach when they could have gone elsewhere? Every student here is a charity case!" How often all of us forget that.

My debt is so great because I have received from so many. So have we all. I am indebted to my parents for things which they did for me that I can still remember and for many more that I can no longer recall. But I am indebted to countless teachers, friends, neighbors, farmers, butchers, bakers, ministers, builders, electricians, plumbers, politicians, and endless others. We all receive so much from so many different hands. I cannot possibly receive all these benefits and sacrifices without a sense of indebtedness and gratitude. Like Paul I must declare: "I am under obligation both to Greeks and to barbarians, both to the wise and to the foolish" (Romans 1:14).

Love involves the gift of receiving. Love is not something that can be demanded, forced, or bribed. I cannot demand that my wife love me. Nor can I make my children love me. I first give love to them, and they receive it from me, and in return they express love to me. Love is a gift. It is a gift given in relationships which cannot be bought or earned.

It is a blessing indeed to receive the grace of God. God's salvation comes as a gift. We cannot earn it nor do we merit it. We receive it as a gift. Only those who have experienced the forgiveness of sins can really understand the significance of receiving. To receive the grace of God is to know the great joy of being accepted by God. Those who have passed through a spiritual experience in which they have moved from darkness to light, from bondage to freedom, from the depths of poverty to the "unsearchable riches in Christ" can know how to give graciously. "Thanks be to God for his inexpressible gift!" (2 Corinthians 9:15). These are the words of Paul who had known great forgiveness. Paul became a great giver because he had received so much. Paul gave thanks to God "without ceasing" and his actions kept peace with his words.

We Christians give of ourselves because we have received so much from God. The extent of God's giving reached to Calvary. Drawn to the love of the Christ who gave His life for us, we seek to follow His lead in sacrificial giving. Our lives have been changed. They have been changed by the very acceptance (receiving) of forgiveness itself, and we are radically different within because of God's loving grace. We give not because we must, but because we want to express our joy at receiving so great a love. We cannot receive God's great gift and keep it to ourselves. We are compelled to share it. As we have received, so we give and share with others. And the paradox is that as we give, we also enable ourselves to receive. "Every one to whom much is given," Jesus said, "of him will much be required" (Luke 12:48).

THE GREATER BLESSING OF GIVING

"It is more blessed to give than to receive." These words from Jesus are at the very heart of His teachings. They are a great living principle which directs His followers to a higher way of life. Even after two thousand years, however, these words still seem to cut against the grain. They sound nice when the minister uses them when the offering is collected for the worship hour, but as a principle for daily living, someone may remark quickly that they seem hopelessly idealistic. It is a hard saying. These words move against the current stream in modern society. Voices by the hundreds or thousands counsel us to get, earn, win, procure, save, and secure. The prudent, thrifty, and industrious individuals are lifted up as models. This sentence sounds unnatural. Why, it strikes at the basic instinct for self-preservation!

Jesus knew that. Like so many of His teachings, this one called His followers to a higher standard than self-centeredness and self-preservation. This sentence is lifted up like a blazing torch in a dark world to shed light on a path that leads away from the crowded streets to a level of walking on a higher road. Jesus knew that this attitude toward life could not be for those who wanted the easy way. He called His disciples to walk in the narrow way which leads to abundant life.

Generosity finds its source in the Christian, not in natural instincts, but arises from within persons who have been redeemed and inspired by God's marvelous grace. The self-giving spirit cannot be lifted out of its environment and be expected to live. It arises out of a life rooted and grounded in the rich soil of forgiveness, thanksgiving, joy, gratitude and commitment. The fine, delicate virtue of self-giving love cannot be grown in lean soil. Rich soil is essential for its survival and growth. Paul's prayer for the early Christians reflected this view.

"And that Christ may dwell in your hearts through faith; that you, being rooted and grounded in love, may have power to comprehend with all the saints what is the breadth and length and height and depth, and to know the love of Christ which surpasses knowledge, that you may be filled with all the fullness of God" (Ephesians 3:17-19). And again he noted: "As therefore you received Christ Jesus the Lord, so live in him, rooted and built up in him and established in the faith, just as you were taught, abounding in thanksgiving" (Colossians 2:6-7).

Many seek to harvest generosity out of meager spiritual soil and they produce a thin level of giving which is done reluctantly and grudgingly. Many of these people give only from a sense of social compulsion. "Others are doing it, and I will be ostracized by my friends and neighbors if I do not." These persons often weigh the possible responses and calculate the reactions of others before they give. There are some whose selfishness has pushed them into being stingy and close-fisted.

Raymond Balcomb wrote about a wealthy man who had never been very generous in his giving. His church was having a building program and the financial campaign committee appointed a special committee to study his case and determine the best way to approach him. When the committee finally visited him, they stated that in light of his resources they were sure he would want to make a substantial contribution to his church.

"I see that you have considered it all quite carefully," he said. "In the course of your investigation did you discover that I have an aged, widowed mother who has no other means of support?" No, they were not aware of that. "Did you know that I have a sister who was left by a drunken husband with five small children and no means of providing for them?" No, they did not know that. "Did you know that I have a brother who was crippled in an accident and will never be able to do another day's work in his life to support himself and his family?" The committee, obviously feeling miserable by now, had to state that they were also unaware of this.

"Well," he exclaimed triumphantly, "I've never done anything for them so why should I do anything for you?"[1]

Why should he? Why should he learn to give? He needs to get outside his selfishness and discover the joy and blessing of helping others in need. He needs to discover the inner peace and sense of genuine accomplishment which comes in giving. Why should he give? He gives so he might experience the rejoinder which is set loose by unselfish acts. He gives to unlock the door of hoarding and keeping to let in the spirit of compassion, love, tenderness, benevolence, and unselfishness. He gives to enlarge his life, to re-define his attitude toward others and himself, to embrace a nobler way of behavior, to multiply the work of his own hands. To give is to experience the higher way of loving. Why should he give? He gives in response to the cries of pain, disease, grief, loneliness, and alienation which have reached his ears. He gives because he has seen the effects of war, hatred, prejudice, injustice, and oppression, and he wants to make a better world. He gives in response to a vision of a different kind of world when sacrificial love is its foundation. He gives because he has learned a more blessed way.

Unfortunately, everyone does not give for noble reasons. Some give out of fear of reprehension, censure, rebuke, embarrassment, or reluctantly. One such man wrote the Internal Revenue Department and explained: "Dear Sir: Five years ago I cheated on my income tax, and I am enclosing twenty-five dollars in cash because I cannot sleep well at nights. If I still can't sleep well at nights, I'll send the remainder." It was unsigned, of course. I wonder how many people spend sleepless nights because of money. Many toss and turn sleeplessly because of the way they earn it, spend it, count it, bank it, bet it, invest it, and borrow it. I wonder how many are sleepless because of the way they give it? "Money as a master is man's worst

---

1   Raymond E. Balcomb, *Stir What You've Got!* Nashville: Abingdon Press, 1968), 50-51.

master," observed George W. Truett. "Money as a servant is one of man's most valuable servants."[1]

At the heart of our problem with giving, and this includes our attitude toward money, but much more is our basic sin of selfishness. Life is looked at too much through the glasses marked *me, mine, my,* and *I.* Giving will always be done reluctantly and grudgingly when it is seen as a threat to what one must give up of his or her own desires.

In the parable of the rich man who wanted to build bigger and better barns (Luke 12:16-21), he is not condemned by Jesus because he was dishonest or heartless. He is called a fool because he wanted to use what he had in a foolish way. He planned to eat, drink, and be merry. In this brief story a dozen words show that the focus of the man was upon himself: "*I* will do this;" "I will store;" "*I* will say;" "*my* crops;" "*my* barns;" "*my* grain;" "*my* goods;" *my* soul." He only thinks about *his* rights, needs, and desires. He was concerned only about himself. The final test for him was not the size of his barns but the quality of his inner life.

But that man has a twin brother and sister on nearly every block, doesn't he? He/she is in our homes, churches, schools, offices, factories, banks, stores, and government. He/she is the officer of our club, the chairman of the board, director of our committees, officer of our finances, and in every place you look. He/she is everywhere. He/she is in each of us.

Self-centeredness eats away at one's personhood, destroying its potential for becoming its real self. The Dead Sea is dead because it has no outlet. Water flows in but cannot flow out. Therefore, it is lifeless. Our lives are like the Dead Sea when we are only on the receiving end and are unwilling to share. We are spiritually dead. A clenched fist never receives; only as a hand opens and gives can it, in turn, receive. This Beatitude challenges the Christian to direct one's life outward and not inward. An old epitaph affirms this truth. "What I kept I lost. What I gave I kept!"

---

1   George W. Truett, *Some Vital Questions* (Grand Rapids, Mich.: Wm. B. Eerdmans, Co., 1946), 35.

A person has reached a level of real maturity when he or she accepts some responsibility for others in society. No one lives as an island apart from the rest of mankind. In 1935 the Mayo brothers gave a generous gift to the University of Minnesota for a graduate medical facility. Dr. William J. Mayo wrote a letter that was sent with the gift. Here is a brief excerpt from the letter: "Our father recognized certain definite social obligations. He believed that any man who had better opportunity than others - greater strength of mind, body, or character, owed something to those who had not been so provided; that is that the important thing in life is not to accomplish for oneself alone, but for each to carry his share of collective responsibility."[1] As Jesus said, "Every one to whom much is given, of him will much be required" (Luke 12:48).

"Humanity always crowds the audience-room when God holds court," Walter Rauschenbusch once wrote.[2] The Christian cannot escape responsibility for reaching out to others. Jesus took the two great Commandments (Leviticus 19:18; Deuteronomy 6:5) and put them together and made them one. "You shall love the Lord your God with all your heart, and with all your soul and with all your mind. This is the great and first commandment. And a second is like it. You shall love your neighbor as yourself" (Matthew 22:37-39). Love toward God and other persons are bound together. The love that we experience in God's grace is indeed an intensely personal matter, but it can never be only a private matter. I am not an isolated ego. Love for God must always issue outward in love toward others. To say "I couldn't care less" about other people and their needs is to walk out of step with Jesus. Our life reflects love toward God by extending love unselfishly toward others. Our religion and morality cannot be separated.

It is impossible to love God in an abstract way. We show our love toward Him in and through the way we relate to other persons. The Epistle First John gives a description of our love toward God.

---

1   Quoted in Ralph W. Sockman, *The Pulpit* (May, 1950), 108.
2   Walter Rauschenbusch, *A Theology for the Social Gospel* (N.Y.: The Macmillan Co., 1917), 48.

"If any one says, 'I love God,' and hates his brother, he is a liar; for he who does not love his brother whom he has seen, cannot love God whom he has not seen. And this commandment we have from him, that he who loves God should love his brother also" (1 John 4:20-21). To say that I love God means little, if I am unwilling to show this love in my attitude and dealing with others.

Our love of God takes shape as we love others in particular places and at specific times. As we give ourselves to others, we give to God. It is more blessed to give because it moves us out of our self-centeredness into the needs of others. In His description of the last judgment, Jesus indicated vividly that the Godlike persons will be those who have demonstrated their love for God by ministering to the hungry, the strangers, the sick, the poor, and others in need (Matthew 25:31-46). "Truly, I say to you, as you did it to one of the least of these my brethren, you did it to me" (v. 40).

Because we Christians have known such magnanimous love, we, too, must love. It will not be easy. To give is costly. Giving costs time, thought, money, commitment, living and sometimes dying. The sacrifices may be large or small. The Christian has learned to love and give even when the recipient cannot reciprocate. Christian giving goes out of its way to help others as God's grace does for us. Jesus called His followers to love those who have not earned or deserved love. This self-giving love challenges us to reach out to the difficult, hostile, unloving, or even our enemies (Luke 6:32-36). This kind of love does not give because it is attracted to these persons. It does not give expecting something in response but gives in order to help the other person. Self-giving love reaches out because there is a need and an opportunity to minister. It does not seek recognition or reward.

A number of years ago, in a church where I was serving as pastor, one of the members took the responsibility of caring for an elderly woman in the congregation who had no family to assist her. This woman was very gracious with both her time and attention. Each week she would buy groceries for her, bake cakes or pies, and would stop by often to talk with her and see if she needed anything. The elderly lady, unfortunately, was a very grouchy and disagreeable person that no one could satisfy very easily. One day, after the generous woman had had a difficult time with the elderly lady, her husband asked her: "Why in the world do you fool with Mrs. Blank? She doesn't appreciate anything you do for her."

"No, she doesn't," the Christian woman responded. "But I don't do it to be appreciated." That is the spirit of this Beatitude. She assisted because she saw a need, and she did not expect a reward. To serve in the Master's name is compensation enough. It is the greater blessing of giving. To give is to receive.

Love cannot exist in a vacuum. If it is real, it will manifest itself in thought and action, reflection and flesh, word and deed. Real love is self-giving, not self-constraining. Real love reaches out; it does not ask to be coddled. Love gives itself. Love merges its being with its action. Love forgets self and extends itself into the needs of others. Love is self-expressing, not self-seeking. The Christian gives not because he or she has to but because they want to. This Christ-like love is not merely a sentiment, but extended hands into the hurt of society. "It is more blessed to give than to receive." This is not just an abstract idea but a concrete principle for living. Is this not Paul's powerful theme in 1 Corinthians 13? Love is at the center of all the Christian's thinking, living, and ministering.

"It is more blessed to give than to receive" because it is more Christ-like than anything we can do. In describing His ministry Jesus declared: "For the Son of man also came not to be served but to serve, and to give his life as a ransom for many" (Mark 10:45). The foundation for this Beatitude grew out of the example of Jesus who gave. God gave in His act of creation. He gave in His incarnation. He gave in love and self-sacrifice. The self-giving principles by which Jesus lived inevitably led to His death. But His death revealed and climaxed the very principles which He had taught. From Bethlehem to Calvary, from His birth to His death, the life of Jesus exemplified the Beatitude, "It is more blessed to give than to receive." Paul expressed it this way, "Though he was rich, yet for your sake he became poor, so that by his poverty you might become rich" (2 Corinthians 8:9). In another place he wrote: "Though he was in the form of God, did not count equality with God a thing to be grasped, but emptied himself, taking the form of a servant, . . . and being found in human form he humbled himself and became obedient unto death, even death on a cross" (Philippians 2:6-8).

One of the most distinctive emphases in the Gospels is the concern and compassion which Jesus showed for the poor, the disadvantaged, and the sinful. Again and again, by word and deed, Jesus crossed the barriers separating sinners from the religious establishment and offered them forgiveness of sin and acceptance with God. He declared that his ministry was "to preach good news to the poor.... To proclaim release to the captives and, . . . to set at liberty those who are oppressed" (Luke 4:18). Jesus moved in and challenged customs and traditions which were put before people. Whenever customs or traditions demeaned or damaged a person, Jesus criticized them. His first priority was persons, not systems. He reached out to the blind, deaf, crippled, sick, and hurting. He touched the leper, the dead, the unclean, the demon possessed, and self-confessed sinners. Jesus touched the untouchable! But He had come to minister – "to give his life a ransom for many." Jesus did not just talk about giving. He lived it. The cross of Christ was the climax of a life which had been giving to others. His death was the logical outcome of the way he had lived — self-giving. "Greater love has no man than this, that a man lay down his life for his friends" (John 15:13). God so loved — what a Giver!

Christians have experienced His forgiveness, known His grace, received His mercy, and welcomed His compassion. For God so loved is a supreme blessing for which the Christian can only say: Thanks be to God for his inexpressible gift!" (2 Corinthians 9:15). But the Christian is obligated to do more than receive God's love. He or she is challenged to love even as he or she has been loved. "This is my commandment," Jesus said, "that you love one another as I have loved you" (John 15:12).

Jesus has called His followers to a higher law than the maxim: "Self-preservation is the first law of nature." Selfishness is self-love misdirected. To love oneself in the biblical sense is to fulfill the potential for which God has created us. Proper self-love demands a healthy respect for one's own personhood. Self-respect arises out of the awareness that we have been created in the "image of God." In the Christian, self-love constantly denies itself so the higher self, which God has called us to be, might grow and advance. "For whoever would save his life," Jesus declared in a paradoxical statement, "will lose it; and whoever loses his life for my sake, he will save it" (Luke 9:24). The emphasis is not on how much a person can *get* out of life but on how much one can *give.* Life is not to be hoarded for self but is to be spent in service for Christ. "The self-sacrifice of the Redeemer was to be the living principle and law of the self-devotion of His people."[1] "It is more blessed to give than to receive." I like even better the translation of this verse by W. O. Carver. "It is blessed rather to be a giver than to be a getter."[2]

When Ernest Hemingway was given the medal for his Nobel Prize for literature, he gave it to a church in Santiago. "You really do not feel you own something," he said, "until you can give it away." Do we really possess anything until we have the courage to give it away? Christ has taught us how to share as we have received the love he lived and died to give us. His call may lead us down familiar streets or along unknown paths. He may challenge us to greet strangers or friends. His way may sometimes be joyful, and at other times difficult. The response may sometimes be rewarded, and on other occasions discouraging. But He has promised to be with us (Matthew 28:20).

Jesse Lyons once told about the discussions which they used to have in Richard Niebuhr's ethics class at Yale Seminary about what a person should do on the ocean if there were only provisions for four people and six people were in a lifeboat. They argued about who should die: the sick, the old, the well, the young? Clark Poling

---

1   Frederick W. Robertson. *Sermons Preached at Brighton* (New York: Harper & Brothers, n. d.), 195.

2   William Owen Carver. *The Acts of the Apostles* (Nashville: Sunday School Board of the SBC, 1916), 207.

was a student in the class, and he debated heatedly the question with the rest. At the sound of the bell, Dr. Niebuhr would say, "We will continue this next time."

During World War II, Clark Poling served as a chaplain on the troop ship, *Dorchester*. On a dark night while the ship was in the mid-Atlantic, a submarine torpedoed the ship, and it began to sink. Clark, along with two Catholic chaplains and a Jewish chaplain, took off their life belts and gave them to others. As the lifeboats shoved off, they knelt in prayer on the deck of the ship. There on the deck of a sinking ship, Poling and three other chaplains gave their answer to the seminary class question. "Our faith," Lyons observed, "is tested, not in textbooks or in words, but when lives are committed."[1]

The way lies before us. Jesus has called us to be men and women of His way. For some it requires the ultimate sacrifice, a life laid down like our Lord. It is a call to a giving life, a sacrificing life. Having received so much from a God who loves so greatly, we, too, are constrained to walk in that self-giving Way. Isaac Watts has written these words of thanksgiving for such amazing love.

> When I survey the wondrous cross,
> On which the Prince of glory died,
> My richest gain I count but loss,
> And pour contempt on all my pride.
>
> Were the whole realm of nature mine,
> That were a present far too small;
> Love so amazing, so divine,
> Demands my soul, my life, my all.[2]

Grant, O God, that our very lives shall reflect a new dedication to You. May our money, time and total life become instruments to bear

1 Jesse Lyons, "These Triumphant Themes." Unpublished sermon delivered at Riverside Church, New York City, on August 24, 1975.

2 Isaac Watts, "When I Survey the Wondrous Cross," *Baptist Hymnal* (Nashville: Convention Press, 1975), 111.

Your love and grace to all persons. May we learn to hear and live by the words of Christ that "it is more blessed to give than to receive." May we learn to mean these words through him who died that we might live. As we give in the name of Jesus Christ, our living Lord. Amen.

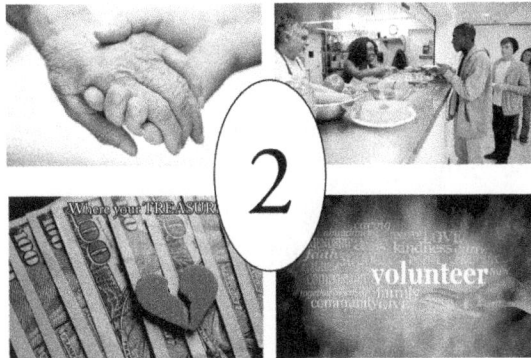

"The Foundation of Christian Fellowship"

Colossians 1:9-22

In the Colossian passage of scripture which was read this morning, we are listening in on Paul's personal prayer for the Colossian church. He is praying that they might know the will of God and be able to follow it. Listen to some of the things he prays for here.

Walk Worthy of the Lord

He prays first that they might "walk worthy of the Lord." It is interesting to note that Paul directs his prayer toward something which is very concrete. Often we think that prayer is supposed to deal with abstract or mystical things that have nothing to do with reality. But Paul prays that the Colossians might have a walk which will be worthy of the God they worship. He prays that their walk might match their talk, and their deeds will reflect their conversation. Sometimes it is easy to talk about God. But it is much more difficult to put those words about God into the reality of one's daily life. Paul prays that what the Colossians say about religion will be realized in the way they relate to others.

A teacher from America went to Africa to teach children. As the Christmas season approached, she explained to her young children the American custom of exchanging gifts. When the Christmas season arrived, one of the children brought her an unusual shell as a gift. The teacher asked the young child, "Where did you get the shell? You must have gone a great distance to find it."

The small child looked at her and said: "Oh, yes, I had to walk to the other side of the island. That is the only place where these shells can be found."

"Oh," she said, "but that was such a long walk!"

"Ah, but teacher," the child responded. "The walk was a part of the gift."

Our walk is always a part of the gift we give to God. Our gift is not merely our money, not just our words. Our whole life illustrates whether or not our words are meaningful. Paul prays that in order to walk worthy of our Lord that the Colossians have fortitude. He prays that their lives might be filled with an inner strength which will enable them to face whatever comes. When they meet difficulties like Paul himself encountered, he hopes they will be able to stand and be counted for Christ. After all, the one writing to the Christians at Colossae had known a great deal of personal difficulties. He was writing them this letter from prison. In another letter Paul wrote to the Corinthians, he indicated that he had been beaten five times and given forty lashes each time. On another occasion he said that he had been beaten with rods three times. He had also been stoned and shipwrecked. His preaching was verified through his living. The two could not be separated. Paul had the inner fortitude to be able to face whatever came along.

In 1 Thessalonians Paul writes to the Christians about his concern that their Christian "walk" had not been pleasing and needed some correction. Belief and ethical behavior are intertwined, Paul was expounding. They are to "walk worthy of the Lord" (1 Thessalonians 2:12). Linda McKinnish Bridges writes that Paul is reminding the Thessalonians that "talking about God is not enough; we are to walk in ways that are pleasing to God… Their walk must match their talk."[1]

---

1   Linda McKinnish Bridges, *1 & 2 Thessalonians: Smyth & Helwys Bible Commentary* (Macon, GA: Smyth & Helwys Publications, 2008), 97.

In Lew Wallace's novel *Ben Hur*, a Roman named Arrius is talking to Ben. "I understand from the hortatory," he says, "that you are a good rower."

"The hortatory is very kind," says Ben.

"Have you seen much service?"

"About three years."

"At the oars?"

"I cannot remember a day of rest from them."

"The labor is hard; few men bear it a year without breaking, and you are but a boy."

"The noble Arrius forgets," Ben responds, "that the spirit has much to do with endurance. By its help the weak sometimes thrive, when the strong perish."

Paul was writing about fortitude — an inner strength which gives the Christian the ability to endure. He prayed that his Christian friends might have it. He also prayed that the Colossian Christians might have patience. We are not very patient people, are we? We want what we want now - instantaneously. But Paul prayed that his Christian friends would be patient. He knew that God sometimes works very slowly to bring about his will.

THE JOY OF CHRIST

Then he prayed that they might know the joy of Christ. This joy is not dependent on external circumstances. It is an internal reality that no one can snatch away from us. The inner joy of knowing Christ sustains us and gives us happiness no matter what the circumstances are.

In Bill Adler's book entitled *Dear Pastor*, a young boy writes: "Dear Pastor, I like to go to church except when there is something better to do." Signed, Teddy, age 10.[1] Teddy reflects an awful lot of us, doesn't he? We talk a great deal about the love of God and how we love his church. It is much easier to speak about Christian joy than it is to live in such a positive way that our lives exhibit the joy

---

1   Bill Adler, *Dear Pastor* (Nashville: Thomas Nelson Publishers, 1980), 1.

we have known in Christ. Sometimes we present a kind of bubbly, superficial happiness but, when any breeze of difficulty blows across our lives, we collapse under its force. We do not have the inner joy to strengthen and sustain us during this conflict. Paul prays that the Colossian Christians might have the inner joy of Christ's fortifying presence.

A Prayer of Thanksgiving

A second stage in his praying is a prayer of thanksgiving. He expresses thanksgiving that the Christians at Colossae are included in those who are now inheritors of God's kingdom. At one time, the Jews thought that only they could be included in God's chosen people. But now, Paul notes, the Gentiles have been given an opportunity to share in the Kingdom of Christ. Through the work of Christ, all persons can share in God's kingdom. Paul lifts his voice in thanksgiving for that fact and encourages the Colossian Christians to do the same. He reminds them that they have been transferred into the Kingdom of Christ. In using this image, he draws on an ancient custom of the conqueror of a city or country to transport his captives back to his own country. When Assyria and Babylon conquered Israel, they transferred the defeated people to Assyria and Babylon. Paul assures the Christians that they have been transported now into the Kingdom of Christ and dwell in his realm. He rejoiced at the rescue which God had brought into their lives.

The Meaning of Being Transported

He informed them that this meant three things. They had been transported, he says, from darkness to light. Christians dwell no longer in the land of shadows. We are no longer caught in a demonic world filled with dangerous creatures lurking in the dark. Christ has brought us into a realm of light. He is the light. He enlightens our every pathway, and we can walk in his light. He has transferred us from slavery to freedom. We are no longer under the bondage of sin that crushes us down and causes us to give way to despair. Now we are persons filled with hope and joy. He has also moved us from condemnation to forgiveness. The grace of Christ has given us a new, abundant, marvelous way of life. Christ has shown us the love of God and his power to forgive sin.

Paul calls upon the Colossians to express thanksgiving to God. Thanksgiving should be the chief source for our stewardship. Because we have received so much from God, we will want to express our thanksgiving to him. Thanksgiving is a genuine part of our worship. Having experienced God's grace, having received so much from him, we declare with a great sense of joy our thanksgiving for what God has done for us. But sometimes we miss this joy, don't we?

A small boy was given some money one day by his father to go see the circus. As was the custom, the circus began with a parade down the street. Down the main street marched the clowns, animals, band and other members of the circus. The young boy watched the parade and was awed by it. When the parade was over, he came back home. His father was very surprised to see him home so soon. He couldn't understand why his son had returned so quickly. "Father," the son said, "it didn't cost me anything to see the circus. I got to see it free." But he had only seen the parade. He had not gone to the circus big top which was set up outside of town. He had only seen the parade.

When I heard that story, I thought about the way many people sometimes participate in the life of the church. They never really experience the joy of the Christian faith. They never express thanksgiving to God, because they have only seen the parade. They have never come into the big top of God's experience to know His grace. They remain on the fringes of the church. They dwell on the edges of the church's ministry, and they want it all for free. They want to stand and watch. They are unwilling to contribute or to be a part of those who sacrifice so the work and ministry of the church can go forward. They observe the parade, step back and enjoy it. They come again and watch the parade as it passes by.

This year your church is calling upon you to be a participant and not just an observer in the ministry of this church. We are calling on not just a few but all persons. We know that all persons cannot give equal gifts. But every person can make an equal sacrifice. Your church needs you to make a sacrifice and not just watch the parade.

Emily and I have wrestled with our own decision about what to do in our commitment for the *Together We Share* program. Before I speak to that, let me go back a few years. I became a Christian when I was fifteen years old. One of the first talks I was asked to give in Training Union was on tithing. I didn't even know how to pronounce tithing much less do it. I remember going to my leader and asking her, "What is tithing?" I did not grow up in a home where tithing was practiced, and I had to learn it from another source. I read some literature I was given and studied the biblical basis for tithing. I remember making a commitment as a young teenager to tithe what little I had to God. Later I stood in Training Union and told those people I was going to make that kind of commitment. I have kept that commitment through the years. We give a tenth of what we make to this church. We have done that in every church we have ever pastored and every church where we have been members. "Scripturally, I do not find anything that would negate the law of the tithe. Many say the tithe is 'old covenant' since Jesus didn't command it," Mike Slaughter observes. "I would argue on the other hand, that Jesus not only expects the tithe but also requires a generosity that exceeds it."[1]

We are going to pledge to the *Together We Share* program this year. We have financial loads just like you do. We have a son in college. We have household expenses like you do. There are things we would like to buy, places we would like to go, and trips we would like to take. But we have decided that this church needs additional sacrifices from us as well. After much prayerful thought, we have decided that we are going to double what we have been giving to

---

1   Mike Slaughter, *The Christian Wallet: Spending, Giving, and Living with a Conscience* (Louisville: Westminster John Knox Press, 2016), 74.

the debt retirement program. It is not going to be easy for us to double what we are giving, but we cannot ask you to make sacrifices if we do not make sacrifices ourselves. We decided long ago that we were not going to watch the parade go by and try to go to church for free. We are going to share in the responsibility of bearing our church's load. Through our giving, we can express our thanksgiving to God. I hope that you will also be willing to make your sacrificial pledge to this program.

A HIGH CHRISTOLOGY

The Apostle Paul continues his prayer for the Colossian Christians and soars to the heights in his lofty words in describing Christ. In this passage we find some of his highest Christology. His emphasis is on the completeness of Christ. He focuses on Christ in creation, and Christ and His Church. He notes the role of Christ in creation as he seeks to confront the heresies of his day. The heresy of Gnosticism asserted that Christ was merely one among the many angels. To them He was not really God's son. He was just one being among all the heavenly creatures on an ascending scale of being. But this was not Paul's view of Christ. He declares that Jesus Christ is the image of the invisible God. The Greek word used for image is *eikon*. He saw Jesus as the expression of God. In Him was the fullness and completeness of God. He was the manifestation or representation of God. When they had seen Jesus Christ, they had seen what God was like. He was like a portrait of God. If you and I look at Christ, we are able to see what God is like.

The Son was the first-born of all creation. First-born was a notation not so much about the one who was first in a time line but was a title of honor. His place with the Father is unique in creation. Paul links Him with the Father in this process. The writer of the Gospel of John declared a similar thought when he wrote: "He was in the beginning with God; all things were made through him, and without him was not anything made that was made" (John 1:3). The Gnostics taught that Jesus was created Himself. Paul challenges this position and indicates that the Son was with the Father in creation. He states that all things were created *by* Him and *for* Him. The goal of creation was to glorify the Son. The world was created that it might bring honor to Him. He is the one, Paul says, who holds all of creation together. Paul declares here that the Son was in the beginning with the Father in creation and is the end of creation. It is the Son who glorifies the Father and who holds creation together by His presence. In these words, Paul has written in a lofty style about the uniqueness of Christ in His relationship to the Father. Leander Keck has given a helpful insight into the concept of the pre-existence of the Son. "What early Christians claimed," he observes, "was that this pre-existing reality became Jesus. They did not hold that Jesus pre-existed; rather what pre-existed was God's Son who became Jesus. All incarnational Christology rests on such a conceptual basis."[1]

A foundational concept of stewardship begins in our understanding of God as Creator. We really do not own anything. Everything belongs to God. As the psalmist says, "The earth is the Lord's and the fullness thereof." All things belong to God. God is the Creator - the source of all life. No matter what we may possess ultimately everything we have comes from God.

A young minister went to his first church. Several Sundays after he arrived, he preached a sermon in which he declared that no one really owns anything. "Everything," he said, "belongs to God." After the service, a very wealthy farmer told him he would like to take him for a ride. He got in the farmer's car, and they rode down the road. The farmer said: "Son, as far as we have been driving along this road, I want you to know that I own all of this. As far as you can see over in this direction, I own all of the cattle. I own all of the houses over on this side." After they had driven around for a long time and pulled up in front of the church, the wealthy man said: "Son, I don't want you ever to preach a sermon again on 'we don't own anything.' I want you to remember everything that I own."

---

1   Leander E. Keck, *Paul and His Letters*, Proclamation Commentaries (Philadelphia: Fortress Press, 1979), 43.

The preacher thought for a moment and then replied: "I'll tell you what I will do. A hundred years from now I want us to meet back here, and then I want you to talk to me about what you own."

We are all just stewards of what we have. No matter how many houses, pieces of property, oil wells, bank accounts, stocks, stores, or crops we may hold, the earth is the Lord's. And we are only stewards of it. We are not owners. We do not really possess these things. A foundational understanding of stewardship begins in our knowledge of God as Creator. To acknowledge God as Creator is to recognize that we are stewards of all that we possess. We are not owners but stewards.

A small girl was turning the pages in a book and marking words she didn't know. She passed over the big word *stewardship*, and her mother stopped her and asked: "Now honey, do you know the meaning of that word?" She looked up at her mother and said, "It means that we may have it, but we are supposed to use it to help others." That was very incisive for a young girl. We may have great possessions, but they are not supposed to be used selfishly for our own ends. All of our possessions are to be used in service for the God we worship.

CHRIST AS HEAD OF THE CHURCH

Paul continues in his soaring praise of Christ and speaks about Christ and his Church. He sees Christ as head of the Church. Just as the human body is powerless without its head, the Church has no power or purpose without Christ as the one who guides and directs it. Christ was the one who began the Church. He was not merely the beginning in the sense that **A** is the first letter of the alphabet or number **1** is the first of the numbers, but He is the first in being the source of the Church. It was out of His life and teaching, out of His death, out of His very being that the Church came into reality. The Son holds all things together by His being. Paul asserts the absolute supremacy of Christ as Lord of the Church. Christ is the one who brings reconciliation and makes men and women right with God. We don't give to try to make things right with God. We give because of what God has already done for us through Jesus Christ. Stewardship does not originate with what we do for God but in response to what God does for us. As the hymn expresses it:

"Love so amazing, so divine,
Demands my soul, my life, my all."

James Denney, the Scottish theologian, once said: "I would like to stand in front of every church and lift up a crucifix and declare: 'He did this for you. Christ died for you and me.'" Having received so much from Christ, how can we take it all for granted without making a commitment to him? Our stewardship arises out of our acknowledgment of God as Creator, out of an acknowledgment of Christ as redeemer, and commitment to him and his Church as the agent of reconciliation.

An interesting exchange occurred in Birmingham, England a number of years ago. A leading department store named *Lewis's* wanted to extend its business on Main Street. But sitting right where they wanted to expand was a small Quaker meeting house. So they wrote them a letter.

"Dear Sirs,

We wish to extend our premises. We see that your building is right in the way. We wish therefore to buy your building and demolish it so that we might expand our store. We will pay you any price you care to name. If you'll name a price we will settle the matter as quickly as possible. Yours sincerely."

A few days later the department store received a letter from the Friends.

"Dear Sirs:

We in the Friends' meeting house note the desire of Lewis's to extend. We observe that our building is right in your way. We would point out, however, that we have been on our site somewhat longer than you have been on yours, and we are determined to stay where we are. We are so determined to stay where we are that we will happily buy Lewis's. If therefore you would like to name a suitable price we will settle the matter as quickly as possible. Signed, Cadbury."

Cadbury happened to be the owner of the large chocolate factories throughout England. He was one of the wealthiest men in all of England. The Cadbury's were also Quakers. They could easily have purchased the department store.[1]

The world is often trying to engulf the Church. The world wants to buy the Church with its trinkets, trades, dances, songs, and ways. But the Church must never be willing to bow down before the material altar of the world. It declares to the world we will reach out and draw you into Christ to reconcile you and make you right with God. Having experienced God's love, we give. We bow our knee before God the Creator and Jesus Christ His Son, our Redeemer. We express thanksgiving in the joy of being able to share in His work here and around the world. May God open our eyes to see what wonders our church can do, when we can learn to respond to Paul's prayer to be persons worthy of the Lord we worship.

O Loving God, we have received so much and often do so little. We have received Your great salvation and often have been unwilling to sacrifice so that others might hear that word. Draw us close to Yourself. In that closeness may our dedication become more real as we sense Your heartbeat pulsating near us and within us. Through Christ our Living Lord we pray. Amen.

---

1   Maxie D. Dunnam, *The Communicator's Commentary* vol. 8 (Waco, Texas: Word Books, 1982), 352-353.

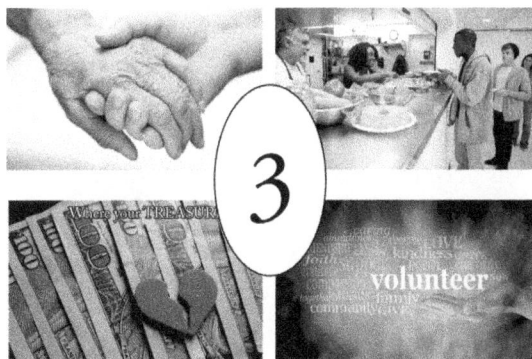

"Now Concerning the Offering"

1 Corinthians 16:1-3

A young minister was at his first church and the time came for the morning offering. As the deacons came forward to receive the offering, he meant to say: "As our Lord has said, 'It is more blessed to give than receive,'" but he nervously said instead: "A fool and his money are soon parted." I suppose, in a sense, both are true. One may be more biblical than the other, though I guess in some ways both are very biblical.

When it comes to talking about a Christian and his or her money, many folks become rather uncomfortable, and they had rather not hear much said on that subject for a number of reasons. One reason is that those who are most uncomfortable with such discussions are usually those who give the least to the church. Sometimes those of us who may give more are still uncomfortable ourselves when we realize the high expectations that the gospels have for us in this area. Off Vancouver there is a spot called "The Zone of Silence." When a ship enters this area it can not receive any sound to warn it of the depth of the waters because the zone is acoustically dead. Many ships have ended up on the rocks there because they could not hear the sounds to warn them of the dangers.

I am convinced that a lot of people live in the zone of silence when it comes to stewardship in our churches. In this area, we are acoustically dead. We really do not want to hear what the scriptures declare about our giving. Some say, "Well, you really ought not to talk about money in church, and especially the preacher. He ought to stay out of those kinds of things, because, after all, that is my private business and not any of his."

That was certainly not true of the Apostle Paul. The Apostle Paul, in the Epistle to the Corinthians, the fifteenth chapter, wrote about one of the most central doctrines of the Christian faith — the Resurrection. We have to remember there were no chapter divisions or verses when Paul wrote this letter. These were added centuries later. Without a moment's hesitation, he moved from writing about the Resurrection of Christ and to flipping over to the other side with: "Now concerning the offering."

From a profound discussion on the resurrection, he moved immediately to writing about the offering. Without a blink of his eye and without sensing a bit of difficulty, he spoke about both because in his mind the two were meshed together. The Christian faith is not totally abstract, unrelated to life and our money. Our faith is very much involved with our possessions.

SPIRITUALIZE THE MATERIAL

Paul was one of those Christian preachers who kept both feet on the ground. Even when he was talking about the Resurrection, he could immediately turn and write about a Christian and his or her money. I think one of the reasons Paul could do this is because he had learned to spiritualize the material. Many people, especially the Greeks, in his day thought that the material body itself and anything material was evil. Since the human body was evil from its creation, one wanted to escape his body and become pure. Even to touch certain things could make one impure. But the Christians, on the other hand, spoke about the human body as the temple of the Holy Spirit. The human body was seen as the habitation of God. God had created his universe and, when God looked upon creation, God didn't say: "It's bad, it's awful." God looked on creation and said, "It is good."

Who owns the earth? Who really possesses the creation which God called good? The Communists say it belongs to the workers. The Socialists say it belongs to the state. The Capitalists say it belongs to those who have enough enterprise and expertise to handle it. Who owns the earth? They are all basically wrong because the earth is the Lord's, and we are all stewards of every single thing we have on the earth. We literally do not own any of it. It is a gift to us from God. We are challenged to use that gift effectively. To do that, we need to learn to spiritualize the material. We need to learn to see within the material realm, the deeper dimension of its possibility of being utilized for God's grace. Our possessions can possess us, or our possessions can become a means. They can become an end in themselves. Our possessions can dominate our lives, and materialism can become the ultimate goal of life. Unfortunately, too many people have been caught up in that approach to life. But our possessions should never be an end in themselves. They should always be seen as a means to some greater goal in our lives. "Lay not up for yourself treasures on earth," Jesus said, "where moth and rust can corrupt but lay up for yourself treasures in heaven." How do you do that? We do that by learning to utilize material things in a spiritual way. We are challenged to use our money, possessions, and whatever we have in such a way that we can glorify God and not permit ourselves to become entrapped by material things.

I had a brief acting career when I was in high school. I took a bit part in a play by James Barrie entitled *The Will.* In this play a young couple come to a lawyer because they wanted to make their will. They had just gotten married, were so much in love, and life was wonderful and marvelous. Philip Ross, of course, wanted to leave everything to his wife and suggested that the will have only one sentence to state this. But she would have none of that. She urged him to leave some of it to his cousins and a convalescent home. They both seem so much in love and unselfish. Twenty years later they come back to the lawyer's office. Philip Ross had now become quite prosperous. Mrs. Ross came with him to make sure that he did not do anything foolish. This time there is much bickering between them, and each spoke about *my* money. The home is excluded. Twenty more years pass. He is now sixty-five and his wife is dead. He comes back to the attorney to draw up his will again. He decides he will not leave any of his money to his relatives, including his children, because they don't deserve to be remembered. As he walks back and forth trying to decide what he will do with his money, he declares: "I leave it — I leave it — my God, I don't know what to do with it!" He moves around anxiously until finally he shouts angrily, "Here are the names of half a dozen men that I fought to get my money. I beat them. Leave it to them with my curses." Here is one whose material goals became an end in themselves and they ended up as a curse and not a blessing. We need to learn to spiritualize the material.

MATERIALIZE THE SPIRITUAL

We also need to materialize the spiritual. Paul did not try to keep his discussion about the resurrection in abstract thought. He used a very earthy metaphor to talk about the resurrection and life eternal. He compared death and resurrection to the planting of grain in the ground. He noted how it is decomposed and, then, is transformed as it comes up through the ground in a new form. You and I too must learn to materialize the spiritual and not keep God off in some abstract place, unrelated to life. We should avoid saying, "Well that's for heaven or that is the spiritual dimension of my life." The Christian faith has been intermeshed by both. One cannot separate his or her spiritual life from one's total life. The spiritual and material are a unit. What we do with our money affects our spiritual life, and how we live spiritually should affect what we do with our possessions. They are both interlocked.

There was a man called Simeon Stylites who lived back in the fourth and fifth centuries. He wanted to be a spiritual man. He built a platform about thirty feet off the ground, and he lived for thirty years on that platform. He never came off that platform but spent his life there in meditation. People would send food and clothing up to him. He was striving to be spiritual, living up there unrelated and uncontaminated by the world, but unknown to him, he was also being very unchristian. Jesus never meant for us to remove ourselves from the world in that sense. He meant for us to be the salt, the light, and the leaven in the world. We are to touch the material dimension of the world and transform it with our spiritual light and life.

William Temple, a famous English theologian, once said that the Christian faith is the most materialistic of all the world's religions. The Christian faith is "the most avowedly materialistic of all the great religions."[1] Christianity doesn't reject, ignore or deny the material. It says that God created the material world, and that the word became flesh. God became incarnate. God came into the world in a unique way and became involved in it, and is not abstract from it. The material life is very much involved in our spiritual life. The Christian faith is not concerned merely with swell ideals or pious abstract contemplations.

A number of years ago in Mexico there was an earthquake which split a church in half. The cross which had been hanging in the back of the church fell down on the floor into all the rubble. One day someone came by the ruined church and saw the cross lying on the ground. They picked up the cross and carried it down into the small town and planted it in the ground in the marketplace. In a real sense, that is where the cross belongs. It should stand right in the marketplaces of life, right in our homes, right in our business, right in the middle of all of our life. The God we worship has become involved in our lives, not separated or isolated from them. He is here in our world. The material is spiritualized by the very presence of the living God in our world.

Notice what Paul says in this passage about the offering. He was concerned here primarily with the offering to be collected for the Jerusalem church which seemed to be in a very bad financial condition. He urged the Corinthians to take up an offering to assist

---

1   William Temple, *Nature, Man and God* (London: Macmillan and Co., 1956), 478.

them. At first he felt that some of his helpers, Timothy, Apollos or some others might take the offering, but he was willing to go himself and ultimately that is what happened. Paul did take the offering to Jerusalem

PRINCIPLES IN THE USE OF OFFERINGS

There are some interesting principles which Paul mentions here that we can use today concerning our own offering. Notice what Paul says. *When* is it supposed to be collected? The offering should be received on the first day of the week when the church gathers together on Sunday. That is the time to give. I have always had a practice whether I received my paycheck weekly, twice a month, or monthly to give every Sunday. This keeps my offering as a part of my worship. Giving is a part of worship. My offering is one way I attempt to honor God. Notice secondly, he says *who* is to give? Each one is to put something aside. It is not reserved just for the wealthy, but every single Christian is to do his or her part. Notice that he tells us *where* it is to be done. "Store it up." Most likely the storehouse is the church. The place for the focus of our giving is the church. We are charged with benevolent work so we might honor God and carry out the ministry of Christ to the needy.

How much are we to give? Paul says it very clearly. As God has prospered us, we give. That doesn't mean that the poorest person in the church should give as much as the wealthiest person. As God has prospered us, we give proportionately. For Paul talk about proportion meant for him the tithe. In the Jewish tradition there was a long history and tradition of returning a tithe unto God. *Why* were they to give? When he came later, he did not want to gather them together and have to beg for more money. There is nothing more tragic than having to beg Christian people to give money for the cause of Christ. Paul says that we should give generously so the church should not have to do that. These simple principles seem valid today

Our Church Offerings

Now, let us look at our own church and the offering. As a church we are at a crossroads. We have gone through a rather tough wilderness. It has been almost three years since our church building burned down. For two and a half years we had to meet in the Seminary Chapel. At least we have come this far, and now we are back here at our place. It is still muddy and messy. The streets in some places are torn up by the city to correct the drainage problem. There always seems to be a mess around here. All of this is a sign that we are getting closer to the end of construction, but we know we have not arrived there yet. What will be our attitude toward our giving as we approach the end of construction? I think we as a church stand at a crossroads. Which way will we turn?

The Temptation of Aloofness

There are many temptations that face us. One of the temptations is *aloofness*. "Well, you know I just am not going to get involved in that. I will just sit back and watch what other folks do." I am aloof from all that is going on. I stand above it. We have some others who are indifferent. They choose not to get involved. "Well, after all I have given my dollar a week for a long time. I am not going to get involved. I will just be indifferent and wait again and see what happens." There are others who will *criticize*. It is easy to criticize the Building Committee, and speak about the slowness of construction. It is easy to criticize why something isn't here and why another isn't there. After all we can't control any of those things, but it is easy to fall into the temptation of criticism.

Other Temptations

Others can fall into the temptation of *ridicule*. They begin to ridicule what one group may have done at church, or they ridicule a leader, or make fun at others or their ideas. Others fall into the temptation of *impatience*. They become so tired of waiting. "After all it has been so long," they say. "When will we ever get it finished?" Impatiently they criticize and ridicule because they are just tired of waiting. All of us at some time or another become impatient. We are too familiar with that temptation. There are others, of course, who fall into the temptation of *discouragement*. Words of discouragement can filter quickly through a congregation and hurts its spirit. Discouragement always raises its head when the times get difficult and the end seems evasive. We can also fall into the temptation of what I call *good intentions*. "Well, I mean to do this," we say, "and one of these days I'm going to get around to it." We have great intentions. It is one of our worst temptations.

I read about a young boy who came to school with a huge paper bag in his hand. The teacher wondered what in the world he had in it, because it looked like an enormous lunch. He continued through the day to hang onto the top of his bag until lunchtime. Finally, the teacher could stand it no longer, and she went over and asked the young boy: "What's in your bag?"

The young boy replied: "blew."

She said, "Beg your pardon. What's in your bag?"

He repeated, "blew. I just blew into it."

There are an awful lot of people who walk around with bags of blew! They have an awful lot of hot air called good intentions which they puffed up to fill "wish bags", but they are not really going to do anything. Sometimes we are all talk but no action.

We can fall into all kinds of temptations and give way to them, or we can begin to see the worthy reasons why we should support our church. I cannot imagine why everyone is not excited about what lies before us as a church. Many of our people are so excited they can hardly control themselves as they see our construction moving closer and closer to being finished. There is much happening at our church which is worthy of your gifts and support. The worship of this congregation is special. The quality and majesty of the worship we will be able to have in our new sanctuary are worthy of your gifts. The music program in this church is worth giving for. The Sunday School ministries and the many learning opportunities in our church are worthy of your gifts. The staff that we have in this church for children, youth, music, education, administration, and counseling and all the other areas are worthy of your support because of the fine work they do. The multitude of ministries we have through our Mission organizations in this church are worthy of your giving. The weekday ministries which we have in this church like the kindergarten, day care, counseling, the job center, the many others are worthy of your giving. The beautiful and functional education building which we have is worthy of your giving. We will have one of the finest worship facilities anywhere; and it is worthy of your gifts. Each of us should be excited about the opportunities which are ours.

Our church is worthy to receive your gifts when we realize how our denomination uses the gifts we give through the Cooperative Baptist Fellowship. Though there are many valid ministries on television, some of these consume an awful lot of our money with few real ministries to show for it. When some of the "television evangelists" were at their height, in one year Oral Roberts received fifty million dollars, Pat Robertson, fifty-eight million, Jim Bakker of the PTL Club fifty-one million, Jerry Falwell fifty million, Billy Graham thirty million, Rex Humbard twenty-five million, Robert Schuller sixteen million, and Herbert W. Armstrong sixty-five million. A total 355 million dollars! Now what do these TV evangelists support? The answer is three churches, five schools, one hospital, and lots of television at an enormous cost.

The Cooperative Baptist Fellowship in the year 2015 received in total receipts from 1800 churches $12.4 million dollars. What did this support? The CBF along with these 1,800 affiliated churches, regional fellowships and ministry partnered with 15 theological schools, 18 autonomous state and regional organizations and more than 150 ministry organizations worldwide, helped found Smyth & Helwys Publishing House and many other ministries. I believe that far more effective ministries are done through the CBF than any television evangelist, and I will encourage my church to support the CBF offering. It's a shame that so much money is often given to these television evangelists that could be used in a far greater way through the CBF.

I am giving my money through my local church. I know where this money goes locally and I know what it supports through my denomination's Cooperative Baptist Fellowship ministry. We have a great opportunity to serve Christ through this church and its ministries and through the CBF. I have had other requests from colleges I attended and other groups that have asked for large sums to support their work. I have made a commitment that while we are in this building program I will not give any large sum outside of my church. This church is my first commitment for my gifts, and I hope it will be your first commitment as well.

We are in a time of great challenge for us. It is easy to sit back and do nothing. This church had a tremendous vision when it decided to build our present building and our new sanctuary. I hope each of us will continue to be caught up in that vision. We have an opportunity to be a great church or an ordinary church. I hope we will give to match our vision - both to support our ministries and our buildings. You can tell what is important in a person's life when you look at his or her check stubs. You can see what is first in a person's life by their check stubs. I am hoping that your check stubs and my check stubs will indicate that we think spiritual things are of first importance. I hope you will let this church be the primary source through which you give your gifts to serve Christ.

GIVING IS A VITAL PART OF WORSHIP

Giving is not a side issue; it is at the center of our worship. Our giving is a reflection of our deeper commitment to God. I hope that next week you will bring your Commitment Card to church which will indicate your deeper commitment to Christ. Let this be your way of indicating that you are making a challenging commitment to stewardship through this church so that God can carry on his ministry here in and through us. The great challenge is before us. I know you want to be a vital part of it.

Helen Hayes in her autobiography entitled *A Gift of Joy* says that she was riding on a train one time and was asked if she would come back and speak with a woman who was dying. Miss Hayes went into this woman's compartment as she could not get out of her bed. While Helen Hayes was talking with this woman, she nodded to her maid to get out a box of jewels. She reached over and took out some gems, and held them up to the light to show off the diamonds and other beautiful gems. For an hour and a half, Helen Hayes said she put on the most marvelous performance of her life as she tried to act as though she were interested in what that person was showing her. As this woman lay dying, all she had to show for her life was some pieces of jewelry which admirers had given her. Her whole life was wrapped up in a diamond studded necklace, some kind of jeweled pen, and bracelet. Miss Hayes said she wanted to cry. It is sad for one to end their life this way.

How tragic it is that too many of us end up focusing our life only on the material, and we do not let the material things of life direct us to God. Paul has reminded us that the offering is related very much to our spiritual life, because it is a reflection of our deeper commitment to God. I hope that my giving and yours will indicate that we are deeply committed to God.

Eternal Father, we acknowledge how easy it is for us to become caught up in material ends. May the material always become for us a means for serving You more effectively. We thank You for having blessed us so bountifully, and now may out of this bounty we give so that others may be blessed. Amen.

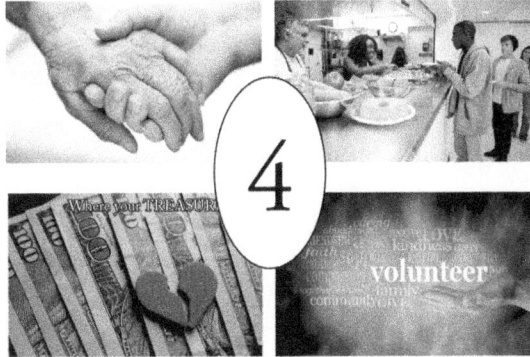

"SMALL IS BEAUTIFUL:
A THEOLOGY OF ENOUGH"

Isaiah 3:13-15; Luke 4:16-21

Several years ago a noted professor was a visiting lecturer at the University of Louisville. He stayed a short distance from the University and traveled back and forth by bus to the campus each day. One day as he waited for his bus, he noticed an elderly woman standing near him. She wore a coat which seemed to have been handed down through several generations. He noticed that her shoes were well worn, and her stockings were disheveled. He thought he could sense something about her poor financial state simply by looking at her. As his bus pulled up, he walked over to the woman, put a $1 bill in her hand, and feeling like he ought to say something, said, "Chin up," and got on the bus. The next day as he waited for his bus, he saw this same woman standing there. As the bus drew near, he saw the woman walk toward him. He thought to himself. "Oh, no. Every day now she is going to come over and try to get some money from me." She walked over to him, stuck a $20 bill in his hand and said, "You were lucky, buddy. 'Chin Up' won twenty to one!"

Sometimes in life everything is not always as it seems. One of the illusions of our culture is that affluence — the making or getting of money — is the primary goal of our life. Many of us have bought into this philosophy. But I am convinced that things are not always as they seem. We are courted by radio, television, the internet, magazines, and newspapers that we are what we buy, eat, drink, wear, drive, or play. How much we have in the bank or how much we spend or where we go determine who we are. We are told that our possessions make us who we are. The illusion is that possessions — things — constitute our authentic personhood. Most of us have accepted too hastily this view as the way of life.

The Scriptures give a clear warning that this is not the meaningful life. Jesus said that a person's life does not consist in the abundance of his or her possessions. The Scriptures point out the dangers of viewing life from the vantage point of things. The illusion of affluence as the meaningful life has been accepted by most persons today.

THE DANGERS OF AFFLUENCE

A pastor approached a church member one day and said, "I understand that you are in real danger."

"I don't know what you are talking about," the man responded. "I have never lived more comfortably. I have more money now that I have ever had in my life. In fact, I never was better in my life."

"Yes, that's what I am talking about," the pastor replied. "I consider any person in your state to be in circumstances of great danger."

SELF-CENTEREDNESS

There are some real dangers of affluence which we often do not take the time to consider. One of these is the danger of self-centeredness. A person with wealth soon begins to think, "I have reached *a* certain standing in life primarily because of what *I* have accomplished." This attitude soon makes us begin to think that we do not need anybody else. What *I* have done, *I* have done on my own. *I* am a self-made person. *I* am completely self-sufficient. Pride begins to control one's life, and its hold echoes throughout all that is done. John Rockefeller was once asked:

"How much wealth does it take to satisfy a man?"

"Just a little more," he responded. Most people always want just a little more than they have. "A little bit more than I have, and I will be secure," a neighbor says. With this perspective, we reach out for more things, and declare by so doing that *I* am what *I* own and whatever *I* have, *I* am. We forget the words of the Scriptures that "The earth is the Lord's and the fullness thereof." We are only stewards of all that we have. We do not really possess anything at all. What I have is not who I am. Even without any possessions, I still am.

A Texan stopped his car one day on a country road in the eastern part of the United States. He rolled down his window and asked a farmer standing in a field nearby: "How much land do you own?" The farmer walked over to him and said, "You see that birch tree over there? If you follow a line from it on down till you come to that wall, then go over to the spring and back up here, that's how much land I own."

"Well," the Texan observed, "do you know that I can get in my car before sunup, and drive and drive and cannot drive across my farm before sundown."

"Yep," the farmer said. "I believe that. I used to have a car like that once myself."

It never dawned on that farmer that anybody could own that much land or should! Too much of life is built on self-centeredness. Many of us are drawn into that way of life out of greed and gluttony.

A FALSE SENSE OF SECURITY

A second danger of the illusion of affluence is that we receive a false sense of security. Our affluence deludes us into thinking that our houses, lands, stocks, bonds, and other material possessions will give ultimate meaning to our lives. Unfortunately, they do not. I have stood by the sick beds of wealthy persons who have found that their possessions could not help them at all in their

time of dying. Howard Hughes was one of the wealthiest men in
the United States. He was a billionaire. But his money turned him
into a recluse. He spent the latter years of his life petrified of germs
and avoiding all contact with other persons. He did not find real
life in all of his millions, but walked down a dead-end street. Many
wealthy people, instead of being happy and satisfied with life, are
discontent, bored, restless, depressed, and looking for that illusive
"something else." Things give a false sense of security. Possessions
in and of themselves cannot give us purpose, meaning, hope, faith,
or God.

You may have heard the legend about the wooden flute which
Moses was supposed to have played when he was a shepherd. Beautiful music was played on it for generations. Then someone began
to feel that a wooden flute was not worthy to acknowledge the
greatness of Moses. The crude instrument was overlaid with gold,
but then it could no longer be played. Our lives can be overlaid
with possessions, and we think we have security. The emphasis on
things has caused us to lose the real values.

Separating Us from God

A third danger in focusing your life on wealth or affluence is
that it may separate you from God. Rather than leading you to
God, the pursuit of money may lead you away from God. Jesus
warned His listeners that it is more difficult for a rich man to enter
the Kingdom of God than for a camel to go through the eye of a
needle. Why did He use this kind of analogy? Jesus knew that a
person could not seek first His Kingdom when He gave His first
priority to things instead of God. We like to think that Jesus is
talking about someone else when He speaks about wealthy people.
But He is addressing every single one of us here. We are wealthy
compared to the rest of the world. Jesus was not talking about a
few millionaires in His reference to those who cannot go through
the eye of the needle. He is talking about you ... you ... you ... and
me. We are wealthy compared to the world's standards.

Do you remember the story about the rich young ruler who came rushing up to Jesus? "What must I do to have eternal life?" he asked. "Go and sell everything you have and come and follow me," Jesus replied. But the rich man went away sorrowful for he had great possessions. In the parable about the rich farmer Jesus told about a man who thought he could build more barns where he could store his wealth and then eat, drink, and take it easy. But at the moment he put his security in his possessions, that night his soul was required of him. Then the question was asked: "Whose now will all of these possessions be?" The late Paul Tillich reminds us that whatever has first place in our life is our god. Sometimes it would appear that we do not own our possessions, but they own us.

The Scriptures warn us again and again about the sin of covetousness. "Thou shall not covet." Coveting extends to not having other gods before Jehovah, not making graven images, not defaulting on an oath in God's name, not cannibalizing the Sabbath, not killing, stealing or giving way to adulterous behavior. At the root of all the commandments is covetousness. If one loves God with all her heart, mind, soul, and strength, then covetousness will fade away. When covetousness is at the center of our life, it crowds out all noble concerns. To love God with all our heart will push covetousness out of our lives. Life does not consist in the abundance of things. Sometimes our things may separate us from God.

Searching for Enough
Strive for a Simpler Lifestyle

I would like to make a plea for a new kind of life — a theology of enough. We need to begin to see life from a perspective other than simply trying to acquire more and more and more. When is enough enough? The first suggestion I would make is that we need to develop a simpler lifestyle. This is a call for moderation. I can remember when my parents got their first automobile. Today most families think they can't exist without at least two cars. Some families have even more than that! Yet most of the people in the world do not have any kind of automobile, and couldn't afford one if they could have it. Instead of one or two suits, or several dresses, many feel they have to have a closet full of them today. How many TV sets do you own? Some have one in several rooms — one for the husband, wife, children and even the dog! Few stir anything manually anymore when they cook. We depend on electric gadgets. We want everything to be electrically power driven, including brushing our teeth. We long for fancier gadgets and more things. Six percent of the world's population in America consumes 40% of the world's goods! Some of the goods which we are consuming cannot be replaced. When the oil on our planet is gone, it cannot be replaced. Ecologists have warned us for years that Americans are consuming more energy and goods than other nations, and we never give it a second thought. In the summertime the air conditioners in the United States consume more energy than all of the energy used in China.

Augustine warned centuries ago that "when my luxury comes about at the cost of my brother's comfort, it is a sin." We need to re-examine the standards, values, and criteria by which we live. Advertising often appeals to our gluttony, pride, ambition, greed, snobbishness or covetousness. Most of the motives are base, immoral, and impure. It should make us uncomfortable to look at the world and the needs around us and realize how little we are doing about it. Advertisements are constantly before us instructing us how we can lose weight. Obesity is symbolic of a lifestyle which is characteristic of a society of consumers. While we consume and grow fat, we ignore most of the world where others are starving to death. And we never even think about them! Is it not time for us to develop a different lifestyle?

Leo Tolstoy wrote a short story entitled *How Much Land Does a Man Need?* A Russian peasant heard about a nobleman who was breaking up his estate and selling small parcels of it. He bought twenty acres of land, and finally was able to call something his own. After a few years, he learned about another region where he could buy more land cheaply. He sold what he had and moved to this area and acquired two hundred acres. He lived there for a few years until he received word that there was another section of land in a distant part of the country where the people were very friendly and one could acquire land very cheaply there. He made a trip to check out the facts, and discovered that this was true.

The tribal chief took a liking to this peasant and made him a generous deal. He was told that for only a thousand rubles, he could have all the land he could walk around from sunup to sundown. Early before dawn the next day, the farmer began walking. He walked such a long distance around the land that he wondered if he could get back before the sun went down. With all of his strength, he struggled back, panting and running until he fell exhausted at the chieftain's feet just as the sun was sinking. When the people rushed over to him to let him know how much land he had acquired, they found him dead from exhaustion. Tolstoy finishes his short story by asking: "How much land does a man need?" The answer was — "Very little — only a plot six feet long and three feet wide — just enough to bury him in."

When will we be satisfied with what we have? When is enough enough? Is it right always to want just a little bit more? Must we always have more and more? Our abuse of the earth's resources may cause others to starve. When our lifestyle affects others negatively, it is wrong and should be changed. We may need to live more simply so others can simply live.

Continue the Ministry of Jesus

Second, as Christians, if we are to adapt to a theology of enough we have to realize that we are called to continue the ministry of Jesus in the world. When Jesus stood before the synagogue in Nazareth and finished reading the Scripture, He said to the people: "This very day the Scripture is fulfilled in your hearing." Jesus said, "I am the embodiment of it." Jesus was not merely announcing God's action, but He was fulfilling it. God, through Christ, has come to end poverty, to end captivity, to end blindness, and to end the brokenness of humanity. But they continue to be with us. Poverty, for example, is still in our world. You and I as Christians are challenged to be vehicles for God to help overcome it. In the Old Testament the poor were the special concern of God. The Hebrew judges were told to give the poor protection (Deuteronomy 16:19). The poor were allowed to glean in the fields and vineyards (Leviticus 19:9-10). Jesus spoke about concern for the poor (Matthew 19:21, John 13:29).

The grip of poverty clasps much of the world. There are people literally starving to death in India, Pakistan, Afghanistan, Africa and other sections of the world. A 2015 report on World Hunger stated that "In the developing world, more than 1.4 billion people currently live below the international poverty line, earning less than $1.25 per day."[1] In his book, *Why Men Rebel,* Ted Gurr has concluded that when people are deprived of their basic human needs or human rights, they are likely to make war or be violent. Without food to eat, men and women will sometimes resort to any means to get this elementary necessity.[2] What kind of judgment is leveled on us when most of the surplus food of the world is stockpiled in the United States? We are reminded of the words of John, "But if anyone has the world's goods and sees his brother in need, yet closes his heart against him, how does God's love abide in him? Little children, let us not love in word or speech, but in deed and truth" (I John 3:17-18).

One of the things we sometimes forget is that there is hunger in America. No matter what government propaganda you read or hear about people in the U.S. being better off today, it is not true. Listen to statistics: 46.7 million Americans — almost 15% of the population — live below the federal poverty line. Just think. 46.7 million people! Children are now the poorest age group in America. One out of every four U.S. children — over 15.5 million — lives in poverty. Almost one-half of America's Black children and one-third

---

1   "World Hunger Facts." www.worldhunger.org
2   Ted Robert Gurr, *Why Men Rebel* (New York: Taylor & Francis, 2010), xff.

of Hispanic children live below the poverty level.[1] This is happening in America, our county, our state, our city and we close our eyes and ignore the problems. We refuse to hear the challenge of Christ to get involved in meeting the needs of people. We continue to accumulate more and more for ourselves and do less and less to meet the needs of others.

There are some who are literally in prison who need to be visited and helped. There are others who are imprisoned by sin. There are some who are literally blind and can be helped by surgery. There are others who are blinded by sin. There are others who are bruised and broken and need somebody to come give them healing and hope. You and I have been commissioned by our Lord to be his instruments in bringing healing to this brokenness. Some of us need to go into our neighborhood and give help. Others can go into our county. Some of us can reach into other parts of North Carolina. Still others may be able to go into needy sections of the United States. We can all give our money to help meet human needs.

In 1923 Japan had a devastating earthquake that left five million people homeless in Tokyo, a hundred thousand dead, and thousands starving. The government did not know what to do. A noted Christian named Kagawa traveled from Kobe to Tokyo to survey the situation. He returned to Kobe, got supplies, clothing, food, bedding and hired a deep sea fishing vessel and sailed up the coast to Tokyo to give aid. He established relief centers where people could go to receive clothing, food, and shelter. He was only one person! Soon the government began to notice the work of Kagawa. They were so impressed by his efforts that the prime minister put him on an imperial economic commission.

Here was one man who had some answers. He was one Christian man who was trying to do something about the problems of his country. Just think what you and I as Christian men and women could do if we joined hands with our fellow Baptists and other Christians of other denominations across our country and across the world to heal the brokenness of humanity. Christ has called

---

1 www.worldhunger.org/articles

us to go into the hurting world and minister in his name. George MacLeod has expressed it well when he wrote: "I am recovering the claim that Jesus was not crucified in a cathedral between two candles, but on a cross between two thieves; on the town garbage heap; at a crossroads so cosmopolitan that they had to write His title in Hebrew and in Latin and in Greek (or shall we say in English, in Bantu, and in Afrikaans?); at the kind of place where cynics talk smut, and thieves curse, and soldiers gamble. Because that is where He died. And that is what He died about. And that is where churchmen should be and what churchmanship should be about."[1]

What Is Success?

I also believe that if we are going to develop a "theology of enough," in the third place, we will have to re-examine our understanding of success. Success must not be judged primarily in terms of what a person has financially. We can't say that a person is successful merely by the fact that he or she has money. We need to judge a person's success from a different perspective — how he or she may serve the church, community, country, or help other people. Many persons have made their contributions to society without money or fame being their motive. Spinoza was one of the great philosophers of all times. His books were very popular in his day. Louis XIV offered Spinoza a pension and patronage if he would dedicate one of his books to him. Spinoza didn't have much money. He earned his living by polishing lenses in Holland. But he didn't like the king and disagreed with his philosophy and ways of government. So he rejected the king's offer and continued to write and polish lenses to make a living.

Albert Schweitzer had achieved success as a theologian, teacher, musician, and philosopher, but he gave it all up to become a medical doctor, and went to Africa to serve Christ in a remote part of the world. Several years ago a young brain surgeon, whose specialty was working with children, left Louisville and went abroad to

---

1   George MacLeod, *Only One Way Left* (Glasgow: The Iona Community, 1956), 38.

serve as a medical missionary in a distant land. He heard the cries of thousands, no — millions, who were without a surgeon. I know young people who have joined the Peace Corps when they could have had lucrative jobs in our country. But they wanted to find a place to serve. I know of men and women who continue to teach in seminaries and colleges at low salaries, who could make much larger incomes in some other professions of life, but they are committed to teaching young people and not in how much money they can make. When Viktor Frankl stood in a German concentration camp, stripped naked, and did not have anything at all, he asked himself in that moment: "Does life have any meaning?" If you had none of your possessions, if you were stripped naked, who would you be then? Can you find fulfillment, meaning, and purpose in some way other than material ends?

POSSESSIONS ARE NOT ENDS

Then finally we need to realize that possessions are not ends in themselves. They are means. God has put us here to be stewards of the earth. We are only managers. "Money is not something I should spend every waking moment thinking or worrying about," Mike Slaughter reminds us. "Money in and of itself is not evil; it is simply provision."[1] When a person dies, often that individual's worth is measured only in terms of money and possessions. As we read about how much an individual left when he died, I sometimes wonder how much he took with him. There are some things you can take with you when you die, but they are not material! We do not take material things into the spiritual realm. Do you give any time to making a life instead of making a living? What earthly good are you doing for heaven's sake? One day I shall die but I shall still have life. "And this is eternal life, that they know Thee the only true God, and Jesus Christ whom thou hast sent" (John 17:3). "I came," Jesus said, "That they may have life, and have it abundantly" (John 10:10). United to him by faith, I have life, eternal

1 Mike Slaughter, *The Christian Wallet: Spending Giving, Living with a Conscience* (Louisville: Westminster John Knox Press, 2016), 205.

life — which cannot be taken away. It is not bought or earned. It is a gift. I receive it.

One day I will stand before God, and I will be judged not by how many possessions I have accumulated. Are you investing your material goods to help others so you can develop some spiritual dividends? The Scriptures declare that I will be judged by whether or not I have served. I will be asked: How many cups of cold water, how many persons in need did I help? You and I have opportunities to share, serve, and minister. Will we focus our lives totally on what we can get instead of on what we can give? **Will** we focus our lives upon accumulating things instead of seeking to find ways to share? Everybody has to have some money to live on, but when is there a point we begin to realize that we cannot keep it all selfishly? We who have need to share. When is enough enough?

Linus, Schroeder and Charlie Brown were talking one day about what they were all taking for "Show and Tell." Linus said, as he held it up, "I'm taking a copy of the Dead Sea Scrolls written in Greek, and I'm going to translate them for the class. And what are you going to show, Schroeder?"

"I'm taking a recording of Beethoven's tenth Sonata in A major and will let the class listen to it and then interpret it for them."

"Fine," Linus says. "And what are you taking, Charlie Brown?"

"I was going to show," as he opened a paper sack, "a red fire truck. But I changed my mind." I want to cry and add another frame which states: "That's OK, Charlie Brown. Show your gift. It's yours and that's enough!"

Each of us is challenged to share his or her gift with God — large or small — offer your best to God. God can and will use it. Life does not consist in the abundance of things. When we sever our relationship with God, we have nothing. When we build our life in a relationship to God, we have everything. John wrote, "This is eternal life, that they may know You the only true God, and Jesus whom You have sent."

Gracious God, too often we have focused upon what we have instead of who we are. Teach us how to live. Make us discontented with being satisfied merely with making a living. Teach us how to live like Christ and to give our lives in Christ-like ministry. For His name's sake and glory, we pray. Amen.

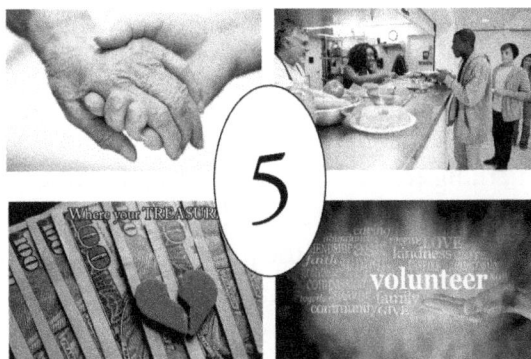

"GIVING AN
ACCEPTABLE OFFERING"

Genesis 4:1-16; Hebrews 11:1-4

It really seems very unfair, doesn't it? Why? Why would Abel be placed in the patron saint's Hall of Fame? Why is he listed with the heroes of the faith in the *Book of Hebrews*? Why Abel? What had Cain done in the offering of his sacrifice that was so bad? It just does not seem fair, does it? Why does God accept Abel's sacrifice and reject Cain's? Obviously, we do not have the whole story in the brief account in Genesis. In telegraph fashion the brief details of the story are set forth. It reads like a parable. Abel's name means vapor, nothingness, or breath; while Cain's name means to get or to create. These two men may be representative persons who suggest something about mankind in their relationship to God and to each other. John Steinbeck's novel, *East of Eden*, places the struggle of Cain and Abel in a modern day conflict.

Why does God accept the sacrifice of one man and reject the offering of the other? Some have speculated that Abel offered a blood sacrifice, and that was the reason his offering was acceptable to God. One can turn to Leviticus and read: "For the life of the flesh is in the blood; and I have given it for you upon the altar to make atonement for your soul; for it is the blood that makes atonement by reason of the life," (Leviticus 17:11). But in the same book other kinds of sacrifices are offered to God and seem to be acceptable to

Him. (See Leviticus 19.) Others have suggested that Abel gave of his first fruits from his fields. Still others have stated that the rejection lay in the motive behind the sacrifices. Abel's sacrifice to God arose out of a sense of gratitude. He sacrificed because he wanted to give something to God. Cain sacrificed because he wanted to get something from God. Abel may have made his offering because he wanted to have a sense of the presence of God in his life. Cain may have made his sacrifice because he wanted to see if he could have God indebted to him.

The writer of the Book of Hebrews gives us a hint. In his roll call of faith, he linked Abel's offering with his motive — a proper faith. In another place in the New Testament — the First Epistle of John, the third chapter, the twelfth verse — the writer, while discussing a Christian's relationship to his brother, asked a question:

"Why did Cain murder his brother? Because his own deeds were evil and his brother's righteous." Wrong and right? In what way? Did the answer lie in the motive? Deep down in Cain's heart, he offered his sacrifice for the wrong reason. Maybe he wanted to see if he could give and then get God obligated to him. We cannot be certain, but this does seem to be at the heart of the problem.

It is clear, however, that at the place of worship — at the altar before God — when Cain found his sacrifice unacceptable, he became angry and in that moment began to plot his brother's death. Just because a man or a woman sits in church does not automatically make him or her righteous before God. In *The Godfather* movie a striking scene occurs at the altar of the church. The godfather stands before the altar as his grandson is christened. The godfather takes a vow to reject Satan and his kingdom. At the very moment he is renouncing Satan; his henchmen are out murdering somebody as they follow his orders. Some can sit in the house of God and their motives and attitudes are not right. Jesus told a parable about a Pharisee and publican "in church." The Pharisee thanked God that he was not like other men. He was proud that he gave tithes and did everything which was right. In his pompous, self-righteous way he went home thinking that he was right before God. The publican, aware of his own sinfulness, left church thinking that he was all wrong. Yet before God the publican was right in his attitude, and the Pharisee was wrong.

It is also interesting to observe that God addressed Cain, not at the altar of the church, but in the field where he was laboring. The church is not the only place where God can speak to us. He speaks to us in our work, in our play, in our homes, and in many other times and places. God confronted Cain and asked: "Where is your brother, Abel?" "I do not know," Cain replied. "Am I my brother's keeper?" Literally he asked, "Am I the shepherd's shepherd?"

Now what has this story got to do with stewardship which is the theme we are focusing on today? I believe that there are some important lessons you and I can draw from this ancient story about our own attitude toward stewardship. Let me enumerate them briefly.

EXAMINE OUR MOTIVES FOR GIVING

First, this ancient story reminds us that we need to examine our motive for giving. Why do you give to God? Why should you give? Some people give primarily out of fear. If they don't give, they think that God might "zap" them. God might punish them or send pain and suffering upon them. Some people give for egotistical reasons. They give to be seen or praised for what they give. Some, thank goodness, give out of a sense of love. They deeply love God. It is unfortunate that many people give for the wrong reasons. Maybe, like Cain, they give to see if they can get a handle on God. They seem to feel that if they give, then God is obligated to take care of their needs and reward them. They say to themselves: "If I give, then maybe I won't get sick," or "If I give, then I will get rich."

A number of years ago the Metropolitan Opera received a check for a hundred thousand dollars. The donor had a slight string on it, however. "I will give you this gift of a hundred thousand dollars," he wrote, "if you will perform my original composition." They examined his composition but found it unworthy of being performed in the Metropolitan Opera. They rejected his composition and returned his check for a hundred thousand dollars.

Do we give to God and put strings on our gifts? Do we give to God and say, "I will give to you and your church, if you will do something for me?" "I will give to the church, if I will get recognition." "I will give to the church, if you will put my name on a brass plaque." "I will give to the church, if you will let everybody know what I have given." Frankly, I do not believe that other people should know what you or I are giving. Our giving is a private matter and does not need public display.

Dostoevsky tells a powerful story about a woman who found herself in hell. She spoke one day with an angel and pleaded that she might be able to leave that place of torment. He informed her that if she could think of anything she had done in her whole life that was unselfish, he might be able to find her a way to escape. She thought for a long time. Then she remembered that she had given a carrot to a beggar one day. The angel told her that he would try to help her. The roof of hell opened and the angel lowered the carrot down on a string to the woman. She grasped it, and the angel slowly began to pull her from the pits of hell. As she began to be lifted, suddenly other people who were also in torment, saw what was happening and they grabbed her legs. They, too, wanted to be free from the torment. As the angel slowly lifted the carrot up, she began to struggle to hold on because of those who were clinging to her. Finally, she cried out: "Let go. This is *MY* carrot." With the word "my," the string broke and she fell back into hell.

Selfish reasons keep us out of God's grace and blessing. We ought to give because we love God. We should give because we have experienced God's magnificent grace. God has freely given His Son that you and I might have life. We give because we have first been loved by God. We give in response to the love which has been given for us. If no one else anywhere knows what we have given, we give because we love God. That should be reason enough.

Give from Our Best

A second lesson we can draw from this story is that we should give from the first fruits of our lives. Each brought, I think, the first fruits of his offering to God. We know that Abel did, and there is nothing in the story to indicate that Cain did not do likewise. In your offering and mine, we ought to give God the first fruits of our possessions. A number of individuals have told me that the first check they write each month is the check for their church. When they get their paycheck, their first thought is, "What can I do for my church?" They give a tenth first out of their love for their church. I wish that I could say that everybody did that in our congregation, but I know better. The size of our offering indicates that is not the case.

A number of years ago a book was published entitled *Magic with Leftovers*. It was about cooking, of course. When I first saw that title, I thought it might be concerned with the financial operation of a church. Too often churches and ministry have to operate on leftovers. Few give their first fruits to the church. Many people drop their offering very casually into the collection plate. Some people are amazed that our church can carry on the ministries it does when they drop only a dollar a week into the offering plate. They cannot believe that all this work can be done on such a small amount of money. Of course, it can't be! Others in the congregation give sacrificially and tithe week after week to carry on these ministries in the name of Christ.

James Cleland, who was Dean of the Chapel at the Duke Divinity School, asked a group of ministers at a conference what was the high point of the worship service for them. Most of the ministers said the sermon. Some said the music. One even said the benediction, which may have reflected his delight that the service was over. If the minister dared to ask the congregation, many might say that was the high point for them. But for a minister that is kind of surprising. But Dr. Cleland indicated that he thought the high point of the worship service was the offering. The offering, according to him, should come at the end of the service. The offering is our response to the preaching of the Word and a symbolic way of giving ourselves. If the offering were taken at the end of the service, our gifts would be in response to the total proclamation of the word of God through music, preaching, praying, and everything else that had happened in the experience of worship. Our giving would be a reflection of our own gratitude to God. Give from the first fruits of your life that you might magnify God.

BE CONCERNED FOR OTHERS

A third lesson we can draw from this story is its focus on our need to be concerned for each other. God asked Cain, "Where is your brother?" "Am I my brother's keeper?" Cain responds with a question. No, you are not your brother's keeper. But you are your brother's brother. You are your brother's sister. This biblical story reminds us that we do not have a private relationship with God. Our experience must be personal, but cannot be private. "Humanity always crowds the audience room when God holds court," wrote Walter Rauschenbusch almost a hundred years ago.[1] You and I cannot assume that we can have a vital relationship with God and be unconcerned with our brothers and sisters in need.

Colin Morris wrote a book several years ago entitled *Include Me Out: The Confessions of an Ecclesiastical Coward.* In the midst of the church's discussion about certain theological issues, he discovered a man lying dead outside his church door in Zambia. When the man's stomach was examined, only a ball of grass and a few leaves were found. This man had starved to death right outside the church while they were debating fine points of theology.[2] The church is busy discussing the difference between Tweedledum and Tweedledee while humanity is dying at its doorstep. What a disgrace for the Church of Christ to spend so much of its time

---

1   Walter Rauschenbusch, *A Theology for the Social Gospel* (New York: The Macmillan Co., 1917), 48.

2   Colin Morris, *Include Me Out: Confessions of an Ecclesiastical Coward* (Nashville: Abingdon Press, 1968), 7.

debating how it will baptize people, or who can come to the Lord's table, or what interpretation of the Scripture is correct, or how it is going to do this or that when humanity is dying all around us and needs to hear the Word of God! You and I in the church need to move East of Eden into the Land of Nod where humanity is and take the Word of God to them. The Church cannot hide in some secluded corner and be indifferent to the cries of pain around it. As we hear their cries, we respond.

I give to my church because it is through the church that the word about the redemption in Jesus Christ is shared with a hurting humanity. I give to the church because it is through the church we reach out to men and women who are hungry and give them bread. If I see a brother or sister who is hungry, and I do not feed him or her, then I am not following the injunction of Jesus Christ. If I see a person who is blind or deaf, and I do not reach out to help him or her, then I am not following the teaching of Jesus Christ. If the church sees needs around it, and does not respond to them and closes its ears to these cries, it is not ministering in the name of Christ. Jesus said His disciples would be praised by God at the Last Judgment by whether they have given food to the hungry, water to the thirsty, and visited those in prison. Through our buildings and a variety of ministries, we seek to show the love and concern of Christ. We give to be a part of that ministry.

If you were standing on the bank of the Ohio River and saw a young child drowning in the cold water, would you not attempt to save him? Hopefully, you would find some way to rescue him. Our church sees much of the humanity around us drowning in sin, despair, loneliness, hopelessness, depression, and hunger. In the name of Christ, we extend them an arm of hope and redemption. We have the means and opportunity to answer their calls for help.

OUR GIFT REFLECTS OUR COMMITMENT TO GOD

The fourth lesson we draw from this story may be the most important of all. This lesson is that our gifts reflect the level of our commitment to God. We can talk about God a lot. We can sing about God or we can study about God. But I am convinced that the bottom line of commitment is reflected in where you and I put our money. If we do not give to Christ's church, it reflects the priorities in our lives. Emerson said the only real gift a man can give is a portion of himself. When you give your monetary gift to God, it needs to be a reflection of the deeper gift of yourself to God. Having given yourself to God, your material gift reveals your love for God. If you love God, you will give to express that love. If love is unexpressed, then one has to question how authentic it is.

I read about a young boy named Robert Hill who was thirteen years old at the time. He heard about the work of Albert Schweitzer when he was a missionary in Africa and became fascinated with Schweitzer. Robert's father was an Army Sergeant in Italy. This young boy decided that he wanted to give something to Dr. Schweitzer, so he bought a bottle of aspirin and asked if one of the planes might drop it off as they flew over Africa. Well, people began to hear about what this young man had done. His effort began with only one bottle of aspirin. Others began to say, "Well, you know, we could give some other medical supplies." Soon the supplies began to swell as others within the military and civilian life contributed to the cause. When they finally arrived in Africa with the medicine, there was one-half ton of medical supplies, valued at over four hundred thousand dollars. All of that originated from one thirteen-year-old boy, who wanted to give something to help the mission cause of Schweitzer in Africa. I am hoping that within our congregation a similar spirit will rise up. I hope it will come from our young people, our older people, and each of us as we respond to the challenge before us. May we be challenged to give and to give generously and graciously. You are important and you are needed.

Our giving is not on the level it should be as a congregation. Our weekly offerings seldom meet the budget. Why? It is hard to say. The spirit in our church is good, but our giving is not what it should be to reflect our love of God. Some think it is because some of our faithful giving members have died. Have others stepped in to take their place? Maybe some of us designate too much of our gifts and do not give to our regular budget. Our regular budget is the basic arm of our church's ministry. Other causes are important but if we fail to support our budget, often our church can't carry on its work. The tithe of every Christian is essential. We all need to give faithfully, carrying our part of the financial load of our church. When we really love God and our church, we will give our proper share.

When I was a young boy, I would cut neighborhood yards to make some spending money. I received the large sum of thirty-five cents. These lawnmowers were the old push mowers without a motor. One day I cut a yard and got my thirty-five cents, and then got on my bicycle and rode up to the five-and-dime store. There I purchased four "silver" salt and pepper shakers for thirty-five cents. Mother's Day was the next day. When I got home, I wrapped the salt and pepper sets in newspaper because I didn't know where any other paper was. I tied a string around them for a bow, and the next day I placed them by my mother's plate for her Mother's Day gift. I remember the nervousness I felt as I watched my mother open that present. It was my first expression of love for my mother which I bought with my own money. But to this day my mother still talks about what my first gift meant to her. It was a small boy's way of expressing his love for his mother. For years those silver plated salt and pepper sets sat beside some of my mother's more valuable sterling pieces. They were given out of my love for her, and she treasured that moment as I do.

I hope that we will give out of love for God. Your gift will symbolize the depth of your commitment to God. Let your motive be right. Give then out of love. Give out of the first fruits of your life. Get your priorities right before God. Through your gifts to your church, you can reach out to the hurting people in the world. Let the gift you give to your church be a reflection of the deeper gift of yourself to him. When Ernest Hemingway received the Nobel Prize, he gave the money away to a church in Santiago with this comment: "A person never owns anything until he is willing to give it away." How much do you own?

O God, who has given us so much, You have loved us beyond our understanding. Your love has been magnanimous and outpouring. Teach us how to love You. May our love be unselfish. May our hearts be filled with gratitude as we learn to give even as we have been given so much. Amen.

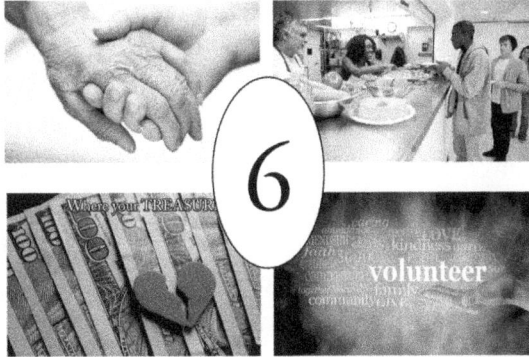

"Sharing Fruit from Your Tree"

Genesis 2:9; Micah 6:6-8
Matthew 26:69-75; Revelation 22:1-2

The Stewardship Council has chosen the tree as a symbol for stewardship this year. In the Book of Genesis, the writer refers to the Tree of Life and the Tree of the Knowledge of Good and Evil. The Garden of Eden story depicts the fall of man/woman as they disobey God. In the Book of Revelation, the writer, John, depicts the restoration of humanity to God in the image of the Tree of Life by the flowing crystal sea in the life after death in the heavenly realm. The Stewardship Council sees three branches on this symbolic tree: "We are called first '*to be*,' then secondly '*to serve*' and finally '*to give*.'" As we look at this theme, I want us to examine the chief leader among the disciples of Jesus, Simon Peter, for guidance in seeing how to apply this theme to our lives.

THE EXAMPLE OF PETER

After the arrest of Jesus, Peter thought that the cause of Jesus was finished. His hopes and dreams about the Kingdom of God had been shattered by the arrest of Jesus. Now he stood in the courtyard below the palace of the High Priest, Caiaphas, and wondered what would happen to Jesus. His heart beat rapidly with fear. His spirit was frozen with terror. He was cold, weary from sleeplessness, frustrated, frightened, and did not know what to do. He moved closer into the crowd of people who were gathered in the courtyard to see if he could learn what was going to happen to the Nazarene. He walked cautiously to a blazer to warm himself from the coldness of the night air. Evidently he had spoken to some of the people in the group around the fire, because they recognized his accent.

One of those in the crowd turned to Peter and asked: "Are you not one of this Galilean's followers?" Peter pleaded ignorance, "I don't know what you are talking about." But the maid servant pressed further. "You are one of His disciples, aren't you? Your speech betrays you." He could not hide the fact that he was from Galilee. The Galilean accent was a thick, heavy burr. He could not deny it. In fact, the accent of the Galilean was considered to be so crude by some Jews that a Galilean was never asked to pronounce the benediction in the synagogue. "You are one of His disciples," the woman exclaimed again. This time Peter cursed and denied that he knew Jesus. Just as he denied Jesus the cock-crow sounded and he looked up, as Luke's gospel records, and he saw Jesus standing on the balcony above. Their eyes met, and Peter went out and wept bitterly.

We usually assume that the cock-crow was the sound of a rooster. But that may not be the case at all. The house of the High Priest was located in the heart of Jerusalem and, according to Jewish laws, poultry would not be allowed in the Holy City. They might defile the holy place. The changing of the Roman guard took place at 3:00 a.m. At the change of the guard, a trumpet sounded to signal that change. This trumpet call was literally called a "cock-crow."[1] At the moment of the sounding of the trumpet and the sentry changed, Peter remembered that our Lord had told him that he would betray Him three times. And he had.

This story is surprising! It is amazing that it is in the New Testament. After all, Peter was a hero and leader in the early church. This story records Peter's absolute failure in the face of his first real

---

1   William Barclay, The *Gospel of Matthew*, vol. 2, (Philadelphia: The Westminster Press, 1958), 382-383.

test in following his Lord. Look at what his story tells us about Peter and ourselves.

DISCOVERING WHAT IT MEANS TO BE

Acknowledging Weakness

This story begins by acknowledging Peter's weakness. This story could be in the New Testament for only one reason. Peter had told it to others. There was no other disciple present that night. Peter was the only disciple that went into the courtyard to see what would happen to Jesus. All the rest of them had fled. Peter had courage enough to risk his own life as he followed his Lord. This story is autobiographical. Peter boldly shared his own failure in the moment of his temptation. But what a testimony it must have been to the early church to know that the one who had been described as a rock had slipped and fallen. If Christ had forgiven him, how much more of an opportunity could there be for others to know forgiveness and experience a new beginning.

Overconfidence

Peter had failed, I believe, because he was overconfident. He had thought that he could withstand whatever came his way. When Jesus predicted the suffering and difficulties which lay before him, Peter stood up and with a ringing cry said: "Lord, if everybody else forsakes you, I never will." He did not recognize his own weakness. We cannot act as though we have no weaknesses. There are temptations which we cannot master with our own resources. We often think that we are tempted at our weakest point, and sometimes we are.

Some of our most devastating temptations, however, confront us at what we think is our greatest strength. Here is a husky male who always brags about his strength and courage. When a fire sweeps through their house, who is it that rushes in and rescues the child? Why, it's the small, weak, timid mother. The husband stands back petrified, unable to move in the face of danger, while she steps forward. A person may appear to be strong, but he or she may not be able to use that strength when it is needed. Our overconfidence may cause us to stumble and fall. Peter did the thing he hated and what he thought he would not do. He meant good but did wrong. When he realized his failure, he fled and wept bitterly. But he did not give way to despair as Judas did and go out and hang himself. His weeping led to repentance and a changed life.

Inappropriate Denial

Peter had denied his Lord, but so have you and so have I. Who among us, at some time or another, through a word, some inappropriate action, something not done or said, has denied our Lord in the office, in the factory, at school, at home, at play or wherever we might be. At some place, at some moment, we have denied our Lord and refused to be His disciple. We were ashamed of the best that we have ever experienced, and we gave in to the lowest dominion in our lives. It is easy to do, isn't it? But the realization that this is possible for us is the first step toward combating the temptations that can drag us down and destroy us.

One Sunday morning as an Episcopal church gathered for worship, a bum stumbled in and sat down on the back pew. The congregation was reciting the general confession. He heard them say: "We have left undone those things which we ought to have done, and we have done those things which we ought not to have done, and there is no health in us." The bum dropped down in the nearest pew and exclaimed, "Obviously, this is my crowd!"

We, like this bum, recognize the truth about our own failures. There are those things which have been left undone, which we needed to do, and there are those things which we have done, and that we have to confess we should not have done. We know we are guilty, and we are ashamed. We have discovered that the power to forgive is not in ourselves. It must come from the Lord. Peter acknowledged his own failure in the courtyard and the forgiving grace of Christ which he later experienced. He repeated this story and told others so they might know about this same kind of forgiveness.

In Aberdeen, Scotland, a noted preacher named Brownlow North was preaching in one of the churches in the city, and right before he was to go into the pulpit, he was handed a letter. The letter was from a man in the city, who recounted a shameful incident in North's past, and told him if he dared to go into the pulpit that day, he was going to rise in the congregation and tell everybody what North had done. Brownlow North had lived a wild life as a young man before he became a Christian. North walked into the pulpit and read the letter to the congregation. He told them that what this man said was true. But he told them about the good news of Jesus Christ that changed his life. He spoke of Christ's forgiveness and how his past was put behind him and he was able to begin a new life. He used his own failure to point other persons to Christ.

The good news this morning for each of us who has sinned is that we can find forgiveness and the possibility of beginning anew in Jesus Christ. Peter was willing to acknowledge his weakness. By acknowledging his failure, he experienced forgiveness.

Accepting the Challenge to Serve

Go another step further and you notice that Peter accepted the challenge which Jesus gave him. In the twenty-first chapter of the Gospel of John, the writer has recorded the experience where Peter and six other disciples met the resurrected Christ on the shore of the Sea of Tiberius. This is the place where Jesus turned to Simon Peter and asked him three times: "Simon, do you love me?" Three times, Peter had denied his Lord, and now three times Jesus asked him, "Peter, do you love me?" The word that Jesus uses for love in Greek asked for a higher spiritual commitment than the responding word for love with which Peter replied.

The questions to Peter seemed to be on a diminishing scale: "Do you love me more than these?" "Do you love me?" "Are you my friend?" On the third time Jesus used Peter's own word for love and asked him if he loved Him even on the level of a friend. "Simon, son of John, are you even my friend at all?" Although painfully aware of his weakness, and deeply grieved at the repetition of the question, Peter avowed that, even though he did once deny his Lord, he affirmed the reality of his love for Jesus. Crying out he declared: "Lord, you know all things, and you know that I love you." Each time Jesus told Peter, "Feed my sheep." "Pastor my people."

Jesus forgave Peter for his denial, and then gave him a challenge and responsibility to go and minister in His name. He had denied his Lord but that was not the end of his life. Jesus forgave him and He entrusted him to serve in His name. Later Peter became one of the great heroes and ministers in the early Christian church. Here was a man whose confidence and self-worth had been devastated in that encounter in the High Priest's courtyard. Peter felt that he had turned his back on his Lord and he had hated the action that he had taken. Like many of us who have sinned, he wished he could undo what he had done, but it was too late. It was over and done.

Experiencing Self-Worth

Sometimes pride can be the factor in our life that pulls us down and destroys us. For others, however, they may have a concept of self-worth that is too low, and this prohibits them from serving in the name of Christ.

Some of us feel like the couple that had gone rowing on a lake in the park one Sunday afternoon. As they were rowing along, Mary reflected on her hope that John was going to ask her to marry him. But he had not said a word. They had been dating for some time, but John had made no proposal of marriage. As John continued rowing on the lake, Mary could stand it no longer and finally said: "John, you know I think we ought to get married." John paused for a moment and said, "Yes, but who would have us?"

There are many of us who struggle with a lack of self-worth. We do not think we are important enough. But Christ comes into your life to tell you that no matter who you are or what you have done, you are a worthy person in His sight. He loves us and wants us to become the best person we can be. God does not ask us to be like Moses, or Paul, or Peter, or someone else. He asks each of us to use the gifts that he or she has in ministry for Him.

I love the marvelous account which Grace Crawford tells about a severely handicapped boy. The first time Miss Crawford visited Michael, he was not able to do much but sit in his wheelchair. He could not sit up unsupported, talk, or use his hands. A year later when she visited him, she discovered that Michael was now able to do some painting and write some. He was also able to do some weaving on a small frame with loops. She saw him pushing his wheelchair into his class and going up to his weaving and hugging it. He knew that there was not a single mistake in it, and it was going to be a gift for home.

A few days before Miss Crawford came was Michael's eleventh birthday. The other kids in his class had sung "Happy Birthday" to him. She congratulated him and told him how happy she was that he was doing so well. He tried to tell her something, but she could not understand what he was saying. Then in a very scribbled way he wrote across a piece of paper the words, "I'm proud of myself!"[1]

In Jesus Christ we find the restoration of real personhood. From our sin we are forgiven and cleansed. We can take pride in who we are because we have the assurance of God's creative and redeeming love. No matter what we may have been or done, Christ can change our life and give us a new beginning through His love. Like Peter we, too, can know forgiveness and the summons to serve our Lord again. We can know what it means to be.

---

1   Robert A. Raines, *Soundings*, (New York: Harper & Row, 1970), 18-19.

A Vision Restored to Serve

Peter also found that his vision was restored. When he started following Jesus Christ, he was among the first of the disciples to commit his life to the Lord. He believed that Jesus Christ was going to usher in the Kingdom of God. He had become a "fisher of men" to help Jesus Christ initiate God's reign. When Jesus was nailed to the cross, Peter thought that his dream was over and done with. But the resurrected Christ restored his dream. Christ forgave Peter for denying Him and gave him a new commission. He restored Peter's vision about the Kingdom of God. Sometimes I see people in church who gave their lives to Christ a long time ago, but their vision has become dull and faded. Their involvement in the work of Christ and His church has become lean. These persons need to recapture their dreams and have their vision restored so they can see once again the possibilities for our world as they serve in Christ's Kingdom.

As many of you know, I am a graduate of the University of Richmond. One of the famous presidents of that school was F. W. Boatwright, who served as president for fifty years. If you ever saw the Walton's program on television, you remember that John Boy went to the Boatwright University. That was the University of Richmond. The television series simply identified it with Boatwright who served as president for so long.

Ted Adams, former pastor of First Baptist Church, Richmond, Virginia, asked Dr. Boatwright one day what was the secret of his life. He replied by telling a story about an experience he had as a boy, when he fell into a storm drain and was carried by the water through an underground channel. Everybody thought he was dead when he was pulled out. They placed him on his bed and began making the funeral arrangements. But he had only been stunned and that night he awoke. He grew up with the conviction that he had been spared for some worthy purpose. This great university stands as a memorial to his dream. He summed up his philosophy in two sentences: "The greatest use you can make of life is to spend it for something that will outlast it," and "whatsoever ye do, do it heartily, as to the Lord ... for ye serve the Lord Christ."[1]

Give yourself to some cause that will outlast you. Give yourself to something more meaningful than just things. Invest your life in the service of Christ and one day you will discover that you have committed your life to something that will still be going on when you die. Peter accepted the challenge of Christ and gave himself to serve in His Kingdom. His vision and dream continues today through your service and mine.

The Call to Commit and Give

Notice finally that Peter *affirmed his faith by his life*. He had denied Christ in the courtyard of the High Priest. When confronted by the maid servant and others, he denied his Christ. Can you not imagine the fear that leapt in Peter's heart the first time the question was asked him: "Are you one of his followers?" He probably wanted to slip into a dark corner or run away. Would you have stayed? Before you condemn Peter for denying Christ, ask yourself whether you would have stayed nearby after Jesus was arrested. You would have to fear not only the crucifixion of Jesus but likely your own death. When he was asked, "Are you not one of his disciples?" he denied it. But he did not run. He stayed nearby in the courtyard. But he had denied Christ with his words and action.

Later after Peter was forgiven and was commissioned into discipleship, he served his Lord through his words, teachings, and even his death. Tradition states that Peter was crucified upside down later in Rome because he did not want to be crucified just like his Lord. Through his words and life, he later demonstrated his faith.

A Tree Is Known by its Fruit

Jesus said, "You will know my disciples by their fruits." "You are living epistles," the New Testament writer wrote of the early

---

1   Theodore F. Adams, *Making the Most of What Life Brings*, (New York: Harper & Brothers, 1957), 127.

Christians, "and you are known and read by others." The way you live demonstrates what kind of Christian faith you have. Jesus' prayer in the Upper Room for His young church was not that God would take them out of the world, but that He would keep them from the evil one. The New Testament scholar, William Barclay makes this observation on the high priestly prayer of Jesus:

Christianity was never meant to withdraw a man from life; it was meant to equip him better for life. Christianity does not offer to release us from problems; it offers us a way to solve our problems. Christianity does not offer us an easy peace; it offers us a triumphant warfare. Christianity does not offer us a life in which troubles are escaped and evaded, it offers us a life in which troubles are faced and conquered ... within the world. Christianity must be lived out. The Christian must never desire to abandon the world, he must always desire to win the world.[1]

Christ has not called us to flee from the world but to live out our faith in the world. It will not always be easy but we have the assurance of His presence with us.

MICAH'S SUMMONS

The passage from Micah 6:6-8 gives us some help here. God has a case to bring against Israel. Micah said that God was holding court for His people Israel. He called them to come into court and plead their case before God. He declared that they have been judged guilty. They were *guilty* of not worshipping God properly. Then Israel pleaded its case, they declared: "We don't understand it. What would satisfy you, God? What do we need to do to set things right?" They thought the answer was in some form of ritual activity in their worship. Micah caricatures the notion by having Israel ask: "Will it satisfy you, God, if we give thousands of rams, and millions of gallons of oil, or even if we sacrifice our firstborn child? Will that satisfy you, God?" But God responds to them: "The answer is not found in ritualistic worship."

1   William Barclay, *The Gospel of John*, vol. 2, (Philadelphia: The Westminster Press, 1956), 252.

Micah then gives a threefold foundation for real religion. *First,* you do justice. You live your life in such a way that you treat others with justice. You cannot gather together in worship and then treat your fellowmen and women in a way that is unjust. That makes worship a mockery. *Second,* he says you will love kindness. You will have your life filled with loving-kindness. Loving-kindness is an attribute of God. He has treated us with loving-kindness and not as we deserve and challenges us to do the same toward others. Like God, you and I will seek what is best for others. And then *third,* you will walk humbly with your God. Your whole life will be lived out in fellowship with Him. Justice and loving-kindness will be practiced daily as we follow God's guidance.

A Faith Practiced

The three points of Micah's message may seem so simple, but reflect on them for a moment. How often is justice not practiced? How often is loving-kindness not a vital part of how we relate to others? How often do we really walk humbly with our God? We are called to authentic religion which is never confined to what happens in this building on Sunday morning. What happens in this building becomes a mockery, if our religion is not lived in our daily lives, and if it is not demonstrated in how we treat other people. The humble walk with God takes on flesh when our religion is seen in everything we do as well as by what we say. You and I are called to serve Christ not merely in a church building on Sunday morning, but we are to live humbly in the world as His servants. The fruits from our Tree of Life must be seen in our living.

Twenty-five years ago First Baptist Church made a decision to remain downtown in Raleigh and worship and serve where we are. Since then the church has engaged in many ministries not only to its own members within but have reached out to many in the community around the church through ministries like the clothing ministry, AIDS Care Team, Angel Tree, Building Together, Children with special Needs, Christmas Breakfast for the Homeless, Emmaus House, Filling in the Gaps, The Gratitude Study Group, Habitat for Humanity, Homeless Bags, Housing Warming project, Infant-Toddler Center, Jubilee Jobs, Meals on Wheels, Mission House for Women, Prayer Shawl, Raleigh Rescue Mission, Salvation Army, Summit House, Support Circle Family, Triangle pastoral Counseling, Weekday Preschool, Wake Interfaith hospitality Network, Urban Ministries, and others. Our church has linked its ministries with many others in seeking to serve Christ here. We serve by giving in practical ways of teaching, singing in choirs, being on committees, worship resource leaders, etc. and through financial giving.

John Killinger, a minister friend of mine, told about an experience a minister, who lived in Spokane, Washington, shared with him. The minister told him about a couple in his church who had inherited a million and a half dollars from an aunt who died. They were stunned. They never dreamed she had so much money.

"This fortune is destroying us," they told him. "We used to enjoy life enormously. We are simple people with simple tastes. Now we have all this money, and it's worrying us to death. What should we do with it?"

"Give it away," the minister said.

"But we can't do that," the couple said.

"You said it's destroying you. You have to give it away."

They agreed to pray about it.

A week later they called him up and asked if they could go out to dinner. They said, "Pastor, we have taken your advice and we are going to give the money away. Here is a list of all the worthy causes we are considering and we would like you to look over the list and give us your opinion."

He looked at the list and said that they were all good causes, "But you have to keep the money." "What was that?" they asked.

"I said, you have to keep the money."

"But you said we have to give it away."

"Ah, yes," said the minister. "That was when you thought the money was yours. Now that you know it isn't, you have to keep it and use it. If you give it all away, it will help the recipients right now. But if you take care of it and act as stewards of it for God, it will go farther and bless more people in the long run."

Then the pastor told Dr. Killinger that this experience had deeply affected him. "I am telling you this because it has changed my life. I now understand what it means to be a steward of the things that belong to God. It means that I am responsible for them all the time. I can't merely give them away and be done with it. I have to handle everything everyday as if it is God's."

Everything we have has to be used for God. Everything! "Handle everything everyday as if it is God's." We are called and commissioned by God to use all we have for Him. We are merely stewards of all we are and have. Like Simon Peter, you and I may deny Christ with our words or lives. We can be ashamed of the highest and best that we have ever experienced from God in His son, Christ, or we can commit our lives to Him and discover what it means to be and how to use everything we have — our life, our strength, our mind, all of our possessions — in service to the very best. Like Peter, we are called to be, to serve and to give. It is a challenge that will always be before you and me as a child of God. I pray that we will learn how to accept that challenge and live effectively because of it.

O God, we acknowledge the power of Your redeeming grace through Christ and the challenge to live by the highest and best we know. This day we commit our lives anew or for the first time to Your service. Through the name of Christ our Lord, we pray. Amen.

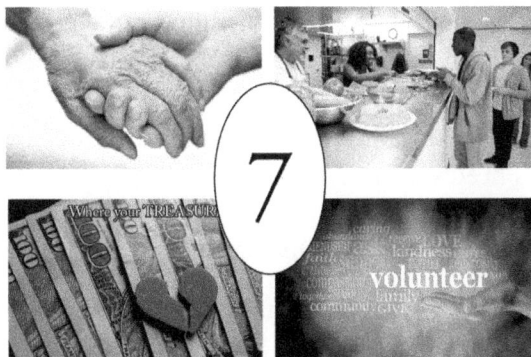

"THE ONE THING WE LACK"

Psalm 52:6-9; Mark 10:17-31

The story of the rich young ruler, the man who came running to Jesus, has been worn smooth with the telling through the centuries. His story is recorded in three of the gospels. Luke tells us that he was a ruler. Matthew records that he was young, and they all three state that he was rich. Unfortunately, this young man has not always received a good press. The ruler has been the whipping boy for a lot of preachers and Bible commentators. How quickly and easily they have said, "We all know what we would have done if we had had that opportunity to respond to our Lord's command." I think that attitude is unfortunate.

TAKING THE INITIATIVE

Let us begin by observing the rich young ruler's approach to Jesus. Notice that he took the initiative. He came to Jesus. Jesus did not seek him. What promise there seemed to be in the fact that he came on his own and running at that. To be seen running would have been considered undignified for a person of his class. We don't know why he was in such a rush. Was he running because he was afraid that he might miss Jesus or was his running a sign of great need or urgency? Luke called him a ruler. Evidently he was a Jewish ruler which meant that he was a man of importance and respect in his community and in the synagogue. The fact that he openly came to Jesus would have brought him condemnation from the religious establishment. Remember that another ruler, Nicodemus, came to see Jesus at night. The young man's coming to Jesus was a courageous act. He was willing even to risk ridicule, because he felt that his need was so significant.

A HUMBLE MAN

He was also a humble man. He knelt in humility at the feet of Jesus. He put his pride aside and pressed his costly robe in the dust as he lifted his eyes to the Master. Kneeling was not a necessary act. It would open him up to scorn, ridicule, and rejection by his peers and maybe others.

A RESPECTFUL PERSON

Notice that he also asked his question in a respectful manner. "Good teacher, what must I do to inherit the kingdom of God?" I do not think this man had evil intentions when he came to Jesus. I think he came in sincerity to Jesus with a legitimate request. He came with eagerness and anticipation in hope that somehow the Lord might have a word of guidance for him.

Unfortunately, as some wealthy people assume, he thought the resources to meet his need lay within himself. "Lord, what must *I do* to inherit the kingdom?" He felt that if he knew what the goal was, he could attain it with his own efforts.

JESUS' RESPONSE

A Question of Sincerity

Move a little further into the story and look at the response of Jesus to the rich young ruler. Jesus first tested his sincerity. "Why do you call me good?" Jesus asked. "There is really none good but God." Jesus seemed to be saying that flattery was not enough. Even eagerness, respect, and emotional desire were not enough. "Stop.

Reflect for a moment and think what is it that you really want? Are you genuinely sincere in your request?" Jesus then reminded him of the commandments. Jesus quoted rather freely from half of the Ten Commandments giving a loose paraphrase of the more practical ones. "Master," the young man responds, "all of these I have kept from my youth up." To us, that might sound like an astonishing claim. But the Jewish rabbis did teach that it was possible for a person to keep the Law.

Lucy in the *Peanuts* comic strip is on her knees praying. "And, I pray," she says, "that I might be a better person ... And that I will get even better ... And better, and better, and better, and ... That's enough!" Most of us can set our own criterion of when our "betterness" is enough. "Lord, I have kept all of these." There are legal requirements which we can all meet if we aspire for them.

Loved Him

Jesus looked on the man and loved him. The word "look" here in Greek is a powerful word. The look of Jesus indicates that he seemed to be probing deeply into the young man's inner being. Jesus looked on this young man and loved him. Why? He saw within this man the kind of potential that He wanted in every disciple — eagerness, discipline, hope, expectation, high qualities, and remarkable gifts. Jesus looked on him and loved him even when he exclaimed: "Lord, I have kept all of these from my youth up."

What He Lacked

But Jesus said to him, "One thing you lack." To the young man, he may have thought that his lack was basically incompleteness. But it was more than that. Oh, we have known persons about whom we have said that. "Oh, isn't he a remarkable person? But he has only one weakness. What an awful temper!" Or, "She is such a remarkable person, so gifted. But if she wasn't such a gossip!"

"One thing you lack," Jesus said. But his demand was not a simple one. "Go and sell all," Jesus said. "Your riches are blocking your relationship with God."

What a simplifier Jesus was. He cut through all the underbrush of minor concerns and focused right at the heart of the young man's problem. Remember that this was not a universal message for every person. Jesus did not require everyone to go and sell whatever he or she had to follow Him. But He knew that this man's primary problem was his possessions. There is no record that He asked this of Mary, Martha, Nicodemus or Zacchaeus. Each had to surrender whatever was keeping him or her from following Jesus. Jesus had told Simon and Andrew, "Throw your nets aside and come, follow me." To Matthew he had said, "Turn away from the tax collector's desk and come, follow me." To some others Jesus said, "You must forsake your father and mother and come after me." But to all those who would come follow Him, He put surrender at the center. His exact prescription was determined by the needs of individuals. Jesus focused pointedly to this man and exclaimed: "Go and sell all that you have and then come, follow me."

FIVE IMPERATIVES

Jesus' second response to the young man is a series of five imperatives. "If you would have eternal life," he said to him, "go, sell, give, come, and follow." All of these were essential if he was to find the kingdom of God. Jesus did not lower His voice to win this man as a disciple. He boldly lifted up the absolute claims of the gospel. "If you would find life," Jesus declared, "this is what you must do."

How differently we often act to reach a rich person for the church. When the disciples saw this wealthy man walking away I wonder if some of them did not pull on the sleeve of the Master and say, "Now, Lord, you have to remember nobody's perfect. We could use that guy." But not Jesus. He does not offer cheap grace. He does not offer bargain-basement religion. The discipleship He demanded could not be bought at a flea market, or a fire sale. His kingdom was depicted as the highest value for which one could aspire and it cost total commitment of life. Jesus was willing to let him turn away rather than lowering Hs standard. To all who would follow Him Jesus demanded: "If you would come after me, deny yourself." "If you want to follow me," Jesus said to the rich young ruler, "then put your riches to help the poor and come, follow me."

A RADICAL DEMAND

Jesus' call to discipleship was a radical demand. He issued a call for total commitment. Jesus always made clear to anyone who was considering becoming His disciple that He understood that sacrifice was a part of His call. He made an absolute claim on His followers. Those who would follow Him had to do so without reservation. The rich young ruler was asked to sell his possessions and give the money to the poor and then to come follow Him. But this was the same kind of demand to which Peter, Andrew, James, and John had responded. These and others had already left all to follow Christ. Jesus' requirement was no less or more for this man.

When the young man asked, "What lack I yet?" he was thrust into making a decision about the man to whom he raised the question. "The answer to the young man's problem is — Jesus Christ," wrote Dietrich Bonhoeffer. "He had hoped to hear the word of the good master, but he now perceives that this word is the Man to whom he had addressed his question. He stands face to face with Jesus, the Son of God: it is the ultimate encounter. It is now only a question of yes or no, of obedience or disobedience."[1]

THE YOUNG MAN'S RESPONSE

Look at the response of the rich young ruler. At the demand of Jesus, his countenance fell and his face grew dark with remorse. He had come with such eagerness and anticipation. The words from Jesus came as an absolute shock. "How could anyone expect

---

1   Dietrich Bonhoeffer, *The Cost of Discipleship,* (London: SCM Press, 1959), 66.

that?" he must have thought. "This requirement is impossible! It is too rigid! It is too ... too much to ask!" We read that he went away sorrowfully. But it is interesting that he didn't go away angry, arrogant, or resentful. He turned away sadly. Does that indicate that there was still a possibility, some slight hope that he yet could be reached by our Lord? We don't know for certain. In this particular instance, however, he was unwilling to pay the price. Do you remember one of the parables of Jesus about a pearl merchant who discovered a pearl which he thought was the best he had ever seen? To have it, he was willing to sell everything he had that he might have this one of great value. Throughout all his teachings, Jesus held up the costly nature of discipleship. For some, they must be willing to sell all to follow Him.

How Does This Relate to You and Me?

Well, I know that as we look toward Pledge Sunday, it is easy to say that this rich young ruler has nothing to do with you or me, because we are not rich. Some of you can say, "I'm not young." Others can say, "I'm no ruler." This story has got to be about somebody else. But I am convinced that the rich young ruler is your mirror and mine. As you and I look into his face, we see our own. Our nation is rich and young. Our nation does exercise ruling power in the world, and you and I are citizens of the wealthiest nation in the world. Today you and I are confronted by the challenge from our Lord on what we need to do with our call to discipleship. What will be your and my response when we ask our Lord, "What do I lack?"

What We Lack

What would our Lord say we still lacked? Would He not say that for many of us grasping is more apparent than giving in our lives? We, like the young man, are more concerned with holding on to what we have than sharing with those in need. In George Frederick Watts' painting of the rich young ruler, a figure wearing a very expensive robe with a velvet and fur trimmed mantle, a costly turban, rings on his fingers and a large gold chain over his shoulder, stands with bowed head and drooping shoulders. Only a small portion of his face is visible. His arm hangs down on his side. There is a note of sadness about him. The fingers on his large hand are stretched out as though they were claws grasping at something. They seemed to be symbolizing his unwillingness to let go of his possessions.

To the observer of the painting, the message is clear. Sometimes abundance does get in our way of finding the abundant life. Sometimes our possessions possess us. Sometimes our preoccupation with things leads us away from spiritual reality. We become enslaved to things. Prestige blinds our perspective. Jesus points us, as He did this man, toward our need to focus our lives in complete surrender to Him. Christian stewardship arises out of a deeper commitment of your life to Christ. If we have surrendered to "follow" Christ, then all we have is dedicated to the work of His Kingdom. Will we ... Will we as a church, like the rich young ruler, turn and walk away sorrowfully from the demands that come to us to meet our spiritual obligations as members of this congregation? Our church has a wide variety of ministries.   I could take a whole sermon merely to list all of the ways we as a congregation engage in ministry. Our building is often open six — sometimes seven days a week-morning, afternoon, and night. Look at a few of our many ministries: Your faithfulness enables us to do mission work in our association, state, nation, and around the world. We support colleges, seminaries, missionaries, and many other causes around the world. We have programs for children, teenagers, and adults. These programs cross all age barriers and reach out to singles and couples. We have music programs, which reach out to children, youth and adults. There are programs of all kinds for children, youth, and the elderly. We have missions and ministries that reach out to our own community, into our state and around the world. These ministries need your support and mine. They cannot survive without our financial commitment.

What Do We Lack as a Church?

The Commitment of All

What do we lack as a church? We lack the commitment of all church members to see their responsibility to bear their part of our church's financial load. When we surrender our lives to Christ, we commit our material gifts to spiritual ends. No one can give when his or her hand is closed. It is only when we open them to meet the needs of others that we really learn to minister.

In Dostoevsky's *Brothers Karamazov* there is a character about whom it was said, "He can be carried off his feet by noble ideals ... if they need not be paid for." Real gratitude seeks to help pay for its responsibilities and ideals. It endeavors to put its money where its mouth is. It doesn't just talk about something, but it makes a commitment of one's stewardship to carry it through. We should be thankful to God and for what this particular local expression of God means in our lives, and so we give cheerfully.

The Encumbrance of Wealth

Secondly, observe that Jesus' commentary on the departure of the rich young ruler points vividly to the burden of riches. Jesus used a rather humorous and exaggerated image to make his point. He stated that it was easier for a camel to go through the eye of a needle than for a rich person to enter the kingdom of God. Various writers who have tried to side-step the impossibility of this figure have missed the point. Jesus was not referring to some small gate which a camel had to stoop down on his knees to get through. Nor can one play around with the Greek word for camel and alter the text to make it refer to a "rope." Jesus spoke literally about the impossibility of some old hump-backed camel trying to poke its huge nose through the small opening of a needle. He was saying clearly that it was impossible. If a person lets his/her wealth get in the way, then that individual cannot enter the kingdom of God. Sometimes our money — our possessions — gets in our way of coming into God's kingdom. Our grasping for things and our desire for absolute security become ends in themselves and bind us to the world.

You may have heard about the small boy who got his hand stuck in his mother's expensive vase. His father struggled for some time to free his son's hand. He instructed him to turn his hand first one way and then another. But the boy could not get it free. Finally, his father took a hammer and was going to bust the expensive vase to free his son's hand. Before he did, he said: "Well, son, let's try one more time. If you will open your hand like this maybe you can pull it free. See if you can do it."

"Oh, but daddy," the boy responded, "If I do that, I'll drop my dime."

There are so many who hold on to material values so firmly that they become our chief end in life. When materialism becomes an end in itself, it blinds us to Christ's call to service. Materialism is a sin when it focuses on itself instead of being seen as a means to a greater good. Money is not evil in and of itself, but the "love of money" is!

LIFE'S ULTIMATE MEANING NOT IN MATERIAL POSSESSIONS

Jesus also reminds us that the ultimate goals and values in life cannot be found in material possessions. It is interesting to note in this story that this young man had plenty of money, yet he came to Jesus to seek something beyond his wealth. He knew that his life still lacked something. A person can have plenty of money and still not have happiness, purpose, or meaning. This young man came to the Lord to discover meaning and direction in his life.

You may have seen or read the play by Tennessee Williams, *Cat on a Hot Tin Roof.* "Big Daddy," the wealthy father, is talking to his son, Brick. His words may express the secret desire of many. "The human animal is a beast that dies and if he's got money he buys and buys and buys," Big Daddy observes. "And I think the reason he buys everything he can buy is that in the back of his mind he has the crazy hope that one of his purchases will be life everlasting, which it can never be. This human animal is a beast."[1]

Too often we simply surround ourselves with things, thinking that through purchasing them, we might have eternal life. But real "life" is not found through what we have. Possessions are only a means toward a greater end. I think we should invest our money, in causes that will outlive us! I want to give to causes that will enrich life and influence others for good. I give through my church because it is the finest way to reach this goal.

In a powerful essay entitled *Things Money Cannot Buy*, Harry Emerson Fosdick wrote these lines:

> I am hoping that someone here may be liberated by this truth from slavery to the economic test as standard and determinative of life. Put it this way: possession is one thing; ownership is another. Some people possess much and own little; some people possess little and own much. Possession concerns things that can be bought and sold; ownership concerns values that money cannot buy. Possession is having a house; ownership is having a home in it. Possession is having a five-hundred-acre estate; ownership is being a real lover of nature. I am not saying these two are unrelated; I am not saying that possession does not matter. I am saying those two things are different. Happy the man who has been inwardly liberated from the too clamorous insistence of possession and who really lives in the wide ranges of spiritual ownership.[2]

What are *you* doing with your possessions? What are *you* doing with your money to help other people and make the world a better place to live? Through your and my commitment to our church budget, you and I have an opportunity to extend our own hands in ministry. Together we can serve God in a way that we can never do by ourselves.

---

1   Tennessee Williams, *Cat On a Hot Tin Roof*, (New York: New Direction Publishers, 1955.)
2   Harry Emerson Fosdick, *What Is Vital in Religion*, (New York: Harper & Brothers, 1955), 173.

If every member in our congregation would catch up his/her tithe, offering, and pledge, we would not have a deficit. You have done that in the past. I know that you can be counted on to do it in the future. Our giving indicates something about our level of commitment to Christ. What a person gives or does not give to the church reveals where his or her real values are. For a person to sit in a service of worship and drop an occasional one dollar bill in the offering plate does not meet your spiritual responsibilities. Many are unwilling to face the reality of where they are spiritually with God. Our giving shows our commitment. Jesus stated clearly that for some people their possessions block their pathway into God's Kingdom. Let your money and possessions be an avenue that enables you to serve Him. Pray that they will not be something that gets in your way.

GOD ALONE JUDGES OUR MOTIVES

Then notice finally that Jesus states that ultimately only God can judge our motives for giving, and God will be the One to reward us. Peter threw up his hands in frustration and said: "Lord, if this wealthy man can't go into heaven, who in the world can?" The Jewish people thought that possessions were a sign of God's approval. If a person were rich, that indicated that God had blessed him. "If this rich man couldn't make it, who could?" Jesus said to Peter: "Don't you worry about it. You have given up all to follow me, and you will have remarkable fellowship in service for me. But you may be persecuted as well." "God often brings about a great reversal," Jesus noted. "The first will be the last, and the last will be first." Who is the greatest in the Kingdom of God? Is it the wealthiest person in the country? We all know that that is not necessarily true at all. How has that individual gotten his wealth; how did he or she earn it? How did he or she use it? What were the causes to which he or she gave it?

Look back through history. Who do we remember? We remember those who gave themselves to causes greater than themselves, who invested themselves in ministry. We remember Moses, but do you remember what Pharaoh's name was? We remember Jesus, but we would never have heard of Pilate, if it had not been for Jesus. We name our children Paul and our dogs Nero. Who can remember the name of the pope before whom Luther stood? God has a way of shifting the balances in history. The greatest in the long perspective are those who serve.

God alone can measure our motives and value to determine our greatness in His kingdom. There are some in this congregation who give sacrificially and who live on small incomes. There are others who make fine salaries who only tip or nod to God occasionally. We need the commitment of all our church members. God has his own "Who's Who." He looks on the heart and knows our motive for giving. Whether our offering is small, like the widow's mite, or large, let it reflect your love and commitment to Christ and His church.

I have never forgotten one of those remarkable stories which came out of the Second World War about Winston Churchill. During this time when the allies did not know whether they would win the war or not, Churchill knew that the only way they could win the war in England was through production. And production depended upon coal. So he called together all the coal miners who gathered in Central Hall across from Westminster Abbey. In this unpublished address, one reads where Churchill spoke frankly to them about the grim and difficult days ahead. But he told them that one day the hand of tyranny would be struck down and they would win. When the war is over and our troops come marching back, he said, they shall march in a great parade through Piccadilly.

As Montgomery leads his troops by, someone will ask, "And what did you do?" And they will say, "We fought at El Alamein." And then the Royal Air Force will march by, that group of few upon whom so many had depended. Then Churchill said a voice will ask them, "And what did you do?" And they will say, "We drove the Luftwaffe out of the sky." And then the Merchant Marines will walk by, that group that challenged the submarine, the sea power of

Germany. Then finally he said there will march by 10,000 begrimed faces of miners with coal lamps on their caps. Someone will turn to them and ask, "And what did you do?" And from 10,000 throats will come the response: "We were deep in the pits with our faces against the coal." We are told that the speech so moved those coal miners, who are not emotional people, that Churchill could not go on. 10,000 of them stood up and cheered uproariously. They saw they were needed and they went down into the pits and they dug coal, and they helped win the war.

Our church needs individuals like you and me in the trenches. Generations from now when our church steeple stands tall against the sky, when our church building stands gleaming in the city, when our programs are amassed and people are involved in ministry of all kinds, you may march by and someone will ask you, "What did you do in the time of crisis for your church?" I hope you can say, "I dug deeply and supported my church. I gave when the need was the greatest. And I gave faithfully to express my love and devotion to Christ."

Who is the greatest in the kingdom of God? The great are those who labor sacrificially for Him. They may serve on front lines, down in the pits, in the back countries, in the jungles, in obscure, unknown places on the other side of town, across the country or around the world. But they serve and give faithfully of their very best to Christ's cause.

There is an old legend which says that the rich young ruler did come back to Jesus. Maybe he did. In the Book of Acts, we read about a man named Barnabas. "And Joses, who by the Apostles was surnamed Barnabas (which is being interpreted, the son of Consolation), a Levite, and of the country of Cyprus, having land, sold it, and brought the money, and laid it at the apostles' feet" (Acts 4:36-37). Maybe ... Maybe he did come back. Could the rich, young ruler have been Barnabas who later served beside Paul in spreading the gospel of Christ to the Gentiles? Christ is still speaking to each of us today. "One thing you lack ... Come, follow me."

Father, grant that we will be willing to surrender self to find the abundant life. Open our mind to Christ's words on the one thing we lack in finding eternal life. Amen.

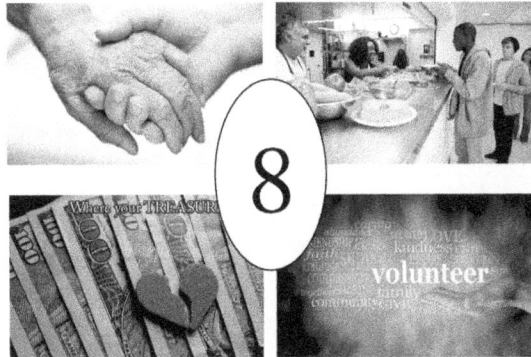

"WITH GOD WE CAN"

Nehemiah 2:17-20; Luke 17:5-10

A man visited the worship service in a church near his home one Sunday morning. When the offering plate came by, he reached in his billfold, took out a bill and dropped it in the plate. A few moments later he noticed that the ushers passed the offering plate again. He reached in his pocket and took out some half-dollars and quarters and dropped them in the plate. It wasn't long, however, until the offering plate came by again. He reached in his pocket and dropped in the change he had left. Later in the service he saw the offering plates being passed another time. A woman, seated near him and who was also a visitor, leaned over to him and asked: "Young man, are they going to search us now?"

Well, there are times in our church life when many wonder, with our special emphasis on stewardship, whether we are going to get to the point of being searched by someone. This morning I do want all of us to do some soul searching about our Christian stewardship. Let us examine the Scriptures to find out what is our responsibility as Christian stewards. We turn to a strange place today to learn about stewardship. We look in the Old Testament at the Book of Nehemiah. The story of Nehemiah took place approximately four hundred and fifty years before Christ was born.

Our hero is a man named Nehemiah, who was a cupbearer in the court of Artaxerxes, the King of Persia. The position of cupbearer was a very important one in this ancient time, because a king was often assassinated by poison. The cupbearer had the responsibility of making sure everything the king ate or drank was safe. The cupbearer put his own life in jeopardy by protecting the king. Although Nehemiah served a Persian king, he was a pious and loyal Jew. Years earlier many of the leading citizens had been taken in captivity to Babylon. By the time of Nehemiah, the Jews had been back in Jerusalem from exile for many years. But the walls around the city of Jerusalem still lay in ruins. His brother, Hanani, brought him distressing news about the danger to the city of Jerusalem because it had no walls to protect the city. In that ancient time the greatest fortification a city had was its walls. Without its walls, Jerusalem was an easy victim for its nearby neighbors who were its enemies.

Nehemiah asked permission from his king to go back to Jerusalem and rebuild the walls. Artaxerxes graciously gave him not only permission to undertake the task but even provided him some funds. He also gave him a royal escort and passports and letters to the officials in Palestine. After traveling a thousand miles, Nehemiah first surveyed the situation, saw what needed to be done, called together the people and then issued a challenge for them to join him in rebuilding the walls. The Jews were pleased with his words of encouragement and agreed to join him in his endeavor to rebuild the fallen walls of Jerusalem.

THE IMPORTANCE OF TOGETHERNESS

Now from this ancient story, I want us to draw some lessons many thousands of years later for our own day and age. The first lesson is this. You note that our text states very clearly in the seventeenth and eighteenth verses that the emphasis is on "Let *us* rebuild the walls." The focus of Nehemiah is on the togetherness of the people. He stressed that it was essential for them to join their ranks to rebuild the walls. Nehemiah did not say," 1 have come to rebuild the walls of Jerusalem by myself," but "Let *us* rebuild the walls!" The people replied, "Let us start the rebuilding. So they set about the work vigorously and to good purpose."

One of the facts in life we all need to discover early in our Christian pilgrimage, if we do not already know it, is that no person can really grow effectively in his or her faith in isolation. Faith does not develop well when it is cut off from others. We need the Christian community. Our community guides and supports us along life's pathway. You and I are a part of St. Matthews Baptist Church because others long before these buildings were built established a church here in this place. Through the teaching, sacrifices and faith of others, you and I can gather here in this place to worship. The Church, as well as this local church, came into being before we came on the scene.

Our own resources individually are never sufficient to sustain this congregation. No one person in this congregation can meet all the needs of this community, whether they be financial, physical or spiritual. We need and learn from each other. All of us are needed to furnish teachers, helpers, committee members, worship leaders, and persons to fulfill all of our mission endeavors. We must never lose sight of each person's importance and involvement in the total life of the church. Too often our focus becomes too narrow and we become concerned only with "my Sunday School class" or "my strength" or "my resources." We then fail to see the larger picture of our church and the total mission and ministry for Christ which we have.

Sometimes our focus becomes so narrow that we are almost like the Midwest farmer who put an ad in his local paper which read: "Man fifty-eight years old would like to marry a woman of thirty who owns a tractor. Please send a picture of the tractor." We can laugh at how narrow this farmer had become. Like that farmer, however, sometimes our focus really can become narrow and distorted. We think that one individual or somebody else will carry our church's financial load for us. Our idea is: "Somebody else in the church will have to take care of things." But each of us needs to see his or her importance and responsibility in bearing the load. The emphasis needs to be placed on "we can." All of us have to be involved in this community of faith. Each of us has a vital part.

Together we can, as we join hands. Our refrain is not just "I" but "we." Our strength is in unity not isolated individualism. It is not in personal "comfort" but in "community." Our strength is not in selfishness, but in the involvement of all of us. Our strength is in fellowship not fragmentation. It is realized not in "I" — isolated individuals — but in "we" — a fellowship of faith where all of us join hands together in our Christian community.

I love the story that took place many years ago in an old theatre which had a pump organ. An organist was playing a concert on the pump organ while a small lad, hidden behind a curtain, was responsible for pumping the organ so it would function. When intermission came, the small boy stuck his head through the curtain near the famous organist and said, "Ain't we great?" The organist in a haughty way, asked: "What do you mean 'we?' I am the organist here." Well, you can almost anticipate what happened. At the end of the intermission, the organist sat down at the keyboards and pressed down on them but nothing happened. He pressed down again, but no sound came from the organ. Then the small boy poked his head through the curtain and asked, "Now who's we?"

Ah, in our churches we need to hear that word again and again, don't we? *We* all are important. Every single individual needs to carry his or her responsibility to make the church work properly. We can't leave the financial responsibility to a few. Each of us has an essential part. It is always asked of us — not equal gifts — but equal sacrifices. We know that all in our church do not make the same salaries. But all of us can do our part and make our sacrifices. Let us join those ancient Jews who told Nehemiah, "Let *us* rebuild together."

STEWARDSHIP TALK OFTEN MEETS OPPOSITION

But notice secondly that soon Nehemiah met opposition. Sanballat, Tobiah, and Geshem began to ridicule Nehemiah and attempted to stir up the people in opposition to him. They accused Nehemiah and the Jews who joined him of rebelling against the king. They did everything they could to bring the work on the wall to an end. In fact, their opposition got so bad that in order for Nehemiah and his men to finish the wall, and they did complete it in fifty-two days, sometimes they had to work with a sword in one hand. But they met the opposition and built the wall.

Anytime there is talk about stewardship in church, there is always some opposition. I have never known it not to happen. The first word of opposition we usually hear is, "We don't want any talk about money in this place." "Money is a private matter between me and God." With a lot of folks, money is more private than sex. They might talk about sex, but they are not going to talk about money, especially what their income is. And they don't want anybody else talking to them about money matters either.

JESUS ADDRESSED THE IMPACT OF MONEY ON OUR LIVES

But read the New Testament. Read the gospels carefully and you will discover that other than the Kingdom of God, Jesus spoke more about money and possessions than any other matter. He doesn't speak about money in some impersonal sense, but he personifies it and gives it spiritual character when he calls it ***mammon.*** Money becomes another god, and this is clearly idolatry. When our money so controls our lives that we don't want anyone to question how we use it, we may need to re-examine our values. Our life can be devoted to only one major end. When money becomes the dominant factor in our life, we do not have room for God. Jesus warned us, "You cannot serve God and money — mammon" (Matthew 6:24). "It is easier," Jesus said, "for a camel to go through the eye of a needle than for a rich person to enter the Kingdom of God" (Matthew 19:24). That ought to scare you and me. It ought to scare us, because we are wealthy beyond most of the world's imagination today. Again Jesus warns us, "Do not lay up for yourselves treasures on earth" (Matthew 6:19). Martin Luther once observed: "There are three conversions necessary: The conversion of the heart, mind, and the purse."

No, Jesus didn't hesitate to talk about money. He told His disciples, "If anyone is going to come after me, let him first count the cost" (Matthew 16:24). Jesus told His disciples that no one was worthy of Him who was not willing to give up everything for Him. If we think money has nothing to do with our relationship with God, we had better read carefully the words of Jesus. He told His followers that they had to be converted from the idolatry of money before they could be His disciple. "Whoever of you does not renounce all that he has cannot be my disciple" (Luke 14:33). When money dominates our life, it has assumed the role of a deity. Our money has to find its rightful place — in surrender to our Lord's service.

You Don't Believe in Pledging?

Another excuse people sometimes use in expressing their opposition to talk about stewardship is, "I don't believe in pledging." Oh, you don't? What you mean is you really don't believe in pledging to the church or God. Who among us doesn't pledge? Have you ever bought a house? Did you pay cash for it? That's highly unlikely. You most probably took out a mortgage. That was a pledge. Do you rent? You made a pledge to come through faithfully with rental money each month. Do you have a telephone or use gas or electricity? If you do, you pledge. You pledge each month that you are faithfully going to pay the bills as they come in. Do you have any credit cards? You pledge.

We all pledge in some way or another. Why do we refuse to pledge to church and God? Without any hesitation, my family and I have faithfully pledged to this church since we have been members here. I have been a tither since I was a teenager, and I didn't earn anything but a small amount of money from part-time jobs. Since coming to this church, we have faithfully given our tithe off the top of our salary before taxes. We have weekly given ten percent of our income to our church from the start of our relationship. Over the last six years since I have been pastor of this church, Emily and I have declined all raises because of the heavy financial load our church has had to bear. We have felt that this could be a part of our gift to the church. We are now going to increase our gift to the "With God We Can" campaign ten percent. This is ten percent over what we had been giving to the debt retirement. This means that we will give five percent of our income to the building program. With this pledge, we will be giving fifteen percent of our income to our church each year.

We have made our pledge and will continue to give it faithfully. We will do this because we believe that this is one way we can show our love to God and our commitment to Him.

Why Have a Banquet?

There are some folks who say, "I don't think we ought to have a banquet. It costs too much." Well, it does cost money. It costs to send you envelopes each month, but we have discovered that if we don't send you envelopes, some of you won't give any offering at all to your church. This year our church, under the fine leadership of Eldred Taylor, has not used any kind of outside resources like we used before from Nashville. Our expenses for this program are going to be half or less than half than what they were this time last time. The banquet is a small investment which stewardship experts have learned is essential. If a church does not have a banquet program where the fellowship, commitment, and enthusiasm is not evident, the giving is always much less in a congregation. Your presence is needed at that banquet, because it is one of the exciting and important occasions where we can verbalize together in fellowship, song, and testimony our commitment.

Why Give to Pay for Buildings?

Well, there are others who sometimes say: "I don't believe in giving to buildings." Well, now dear friends, let me tell you if all I thought we were doing was giving to a building, I wouldn't give a cent. I wouldn't, for a moment, invest the kind of money I do from my own salary just to a building. But I give because of what these buildings represent! The buildings are not ends in themselves. We are not giving to a museum but to mission. We are not giving just for comfort but for a commission. We are not giving so people can be apathetic but so there can be action. We are concerned with salvation not success, service not selfishness, a covenant not a contract. These buildings symbolize worship, praise, ministry and service to God.

When I was a student in seminary, one of the thoughts that my Philosophy of Religion professor shared with us that I have never forgotten, originated from an English philosopher, A. M. Fairbairn. "Every idea has to have some institutional form." You can't have some idea without it taking flesh somewhere. The church needs a building through which its work can be accomplished. If anyone should know that, you and I should! When we didn't have a place for three years after our buildings burned down, we knew the pain of not having a place of our own. Think what a vacuum it made when we did not have a place. But this place makes all of the difference in the world in our being able to function as a church. I give to our building retirement program not as an end in itself, but because of the missionary purposes and worship that it affords. In these buildings all kinds of ministries are carried on every day. I won't list all of these programs again. You have heard about them so many times. In the morning, afternoon, and evening, programs and ministries of all kinds meet in this church building.

A strong base is essential to a church's effective ministry. Last Sunday night we ordained Bob Fox, Jr. to the gospel ministry. He grew up in this church and felt a call from God to ministry. That call was a result of the impact lay persons in this church had on his life as a child and teenager. Two or three Sundays ago a woman and her husband, whom I did not know, walked out of the front door of our church. The woman told me that when she and her husband were students at Southern Seminary, they worshipped one Sunday at St. Matthews. They were not members of our church, but during a service of worship here, they dedicated their lives to go to the mission field. She and her husband served for thirty years on the mission field. That commitment was made in this church. We have witnessed public professions of faith by young people and adults. I have received letters and telephone calls from persons who stated the difference that worship, music, praise, Sunday School, and other programs and ministries in this church-this building — have made in their lives. I don't give to support a building, but to support what goes on in it.

When we were at St. Andrews, Scotland several years ago, we saw the ruins of a giant cathedral standing at the edge of the city overlooking the sea. It had been destroyed by fire hundreds of years ago. The people never rebuilt it. Today you can walk around in the midst of the ruins. But what good are they? Our building burned down. We rebuilt! We rebuilt because we wanted to get on with ministry and worship. That's a reason to give.

A SENSE OF MISSION

Go with me briefly one step further. Notice that Nehemiah told them that he was rebuilding the walls "with a sense of mission." He says in the twentieth verse: "The God of heaven will give us success. We are his servants." Now some translators unfortunately use the translation that "God will prosper us." I don't think we give to get rich. Nehemiah was saying that God was with him. He had a sense of mission from God. We acknowledge through our giving that God is the creator of all of life. We are stewards of what God has given us in His world. We use our possessions to honor and glorify God through everything we have and do.

Our goal as a Christian is to let Christ control our lives. We pray for Christ to control our mind, motives, methods, moods, and money. Do you remember Malachi's question: "Will a man rob God?" He states that God says: "Trust me, try me; prove me." What is the prophet telling us about God? I think he may be saying that the greatest argument for God is not necessarily philosophical or theological. The greatest argument for God in your life and mine may be economic. You demonstrate your love for God by how you use your money. This will be demonstrated not merely by what you give to our church, but how you use your money in everything else that you do. Your giving demonstrates whether or not God is important to you. We are called to serve him. Our proper use of money is one way we serve God.

All of us have many demands upon us from people who want us to give to varied causes. Every once in a while Emily and I give to one of the agencies that ask us for old clothes, old furniture, and the like. On occasions we will put some items out on our porch and later someone will come by and pick them up. But I will be honest with you, we don't give much thought to those items. I know it wasn't any sacrifice to give up old clothes and old furniture. That donation didn't really cost me anything. After all, we wanted to get rid of those items. Thank goodness there is somebody who will come by my home, pick up these items and put them to good use. Is that sacrifice? No, not really.

There are a lot of persons in this congregation who have made tremendous sacrifices for our church and I praise God for them. I know of a retired man who does odd jobs for people — carpentry, cutting grass, or raking leaves. The money he gets from those odd jobs, he gives to his church. I know another retired man, now dead, who was a mechanic. He had been retired for years, but he continued to repair cars. All the money he got from his repairs, he gave to his church. He felt that he didn't need this extra money to live on, and so he gave it to his church. Others in this congregation have told me that they have remembered our church in their will. Others have doubled their commitment to our church's debt retirement program, because they love our church. They show their involvement through what they give.

DOING OUR DUTY

The passage from Luke's gospel in our text recounts one of Jesus' parables about a slave who has worked in the fields all day long and is tired and weary and wants to come home and eat his meal and rest. Because he is a slave, however, he must first go home and serve his master *his* meal and take care of him before he can eat. Jesus says that after the slave has done everything for his master, he knows he has not done anything but his duty. You and I need to realize that no matter what we do or give to God, it is merely our Christian duty.[1] No person can ever outgive God. None of us can ever buy God, bribe Him, or manipulate Him through our giving. All of our gifts are expressions, hopefully, of our love and devotion to God.

I cannot present the Christian faith as an easygoing get-rich scheme. This morning I am not going to tell you for a moment that if you will give faithfully to your church and if you will give to our "With God We Can" campaign that God is going to give you everything you want in life and make you wealthy and healthy. I cannot tell you that God will grant every ambition you want or give you every desire of your heart. I don't believe that is true at all. All you have to do is look at the gospels and observe that Jesus Christ, God's son, died on a cross. Paul, who had committed his all to follow Jesus Christ, was beaten, stoned and imprisoned.

I do know that if you and I give our resources faithfully to God, we will find a blessing that we will never know in any other way. James Denney, the Scottish theologian, used to say, "I wish I could go into every church and lift high the crucifix of Christ and say, 'This is how much God loved you!' Respond to it." God loved us so much that Christ died on the cross for us. Let us express our love by being faithful in all that we give to him. The way of Christ is demanding and costly. It costs time, energy and money. The hymn writer has expressed it this way:

> Were the whole realm of Nature mine,
> That were a present far too small;
> Love so amazing, so divine,
> Demands my soul, my life, my all.

---

1 Justo L. Gonzalez, *Luke, Belief: A Theological Commentary on the Bible* (Louisville: Westminster John Knox Press, 2010), 202.

Eternal God, Your love is amazing beyond our understanding, and we thank You for it. Teach us, O Lord, how to be faithful and to know that we can do all things with You. May we learn through the death of Your Son what a great sacrifice You have made for us. May we willingly, lovingly, and sacrificially, give in return the very best that we can to You. Through Christ our Lord, we pray. Amen.

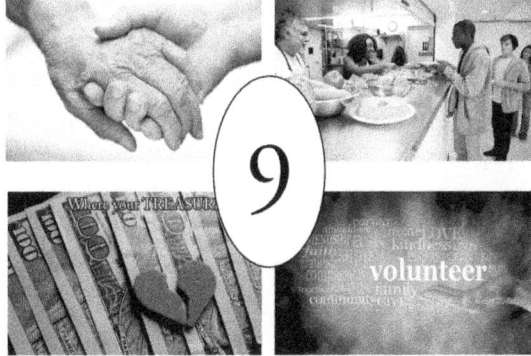

"The Best Things in Life Are not Free"

2 Samuel 24:20-25; 1 Timothy 6:6-10

When I was much younger, I remember a song that used to be sung occasionally which I would hear over the radio or on records: *The Best Things in Life Are Free*. This song affirmed that the moon above, the skies, the birds, and the one I love are free. But we have learned very quickly that the sky, the rivers, the oceans, the sea, and the birds are very costly. What our modern world has done through pollution alone has already begun to erode away the life of these arenas. When we lived in Louisiana, we learned that the pelican was the state bird and that insecticides, which had been dumped into the rivers had killed off this bird. The Louisiana state bird had disappeared because too many thought that the birds, sky and rivers were free.

THE BEST THINGS ARE REALLY NOT FREE

We learn that love is not really free. It, too, is very costly. We have to work at relationships. We have to show love, attention, care, and concern. Relationships are not really free of time, effort, energy, or money. We learn that even friendship is also not free because friends are those to whom we will give time to listen, encouragement, support, understanding, and sometimes money.

When we are really honest deep down inside of us, we begin to realize that the best things in life are really not free. They are indeed costly. Too many people want their religion free. We say that salvation is by the grace of God. We do not have to work to merit it nor earn it, and that is true. But no one really understands the gospel message clearly at all who does not hear Jesus Christ speak about the costly nature of discipleship. He reminds us that if any person will come after Him, let him or her deny himself or herself and take up one's cross and follow Him. It is costly to be a disciple of Jesus Christ. It costs you the commitment of your life and your loyalties to the Christ.

The Dangers of the Love of Money

In Paul's first letter to Timothy, he warns him about the dangers of the lack of a solid commitment to Christ which exposes one to the dangers of money that can cause one "to wander away from the faith." He does not say that money in itself is evil, but "the love of money is the root of all kinds of evil." He encourages him and others in the church to strive for godliness and contentment in their lives. He reminds them that they "brought nothing into the world, and they would take nothing out of the world." The temptation of money has indeed led many persons into all kinds of ruin and destruction. The "love of money" has caused too many to fall into many kinds of ruinous practices such as political bribes, gambling, racial hatred, improper insurance transactions, housing, banking loans and other financial affairs, slum housing, false advertizing, corruption in many areas, and countless other ways that we can not even begin to imagine.

Jesus told us that "where your treasure is there will be your heart." The heart symbolizes in biblical thought the very essence of what constitutes our inner self. "Where your treasure is there will be your heart." And the reverse is also true, I think, "Where your heart is there will be your treasure." What is your treasure? Your treasure is whatever is the most important thing in your life. Our treasures are those things to which we commit our time, effort, and energy. Jesus warns us, "Lay not up for yourselves riches or treasures which cannot be carried beyond this world." Paul is echoing the words of our Lord warning us not to become entrapped by worldly possessions.

When Phillip Guedalla was writing a biography of the Duke of Wellington, he wanted to see if he could perceive the inner self of the man, what his character was really like. Do you know where he went to determine the man's real character? He went to the Duke's check stubs to examine where the man spent his money. He looked at the stubs to see where his real loyalties lay, because he knew that one gives his money to those things which are the most important to him. I wonder what our check stubs would reveal about you and about me. If we give one percent of our money to the church, and for some people that would be a colossal increase, and then, we use ten percent of our money to buy cigarettes, drink, luxuries, and pleasure, where is our basic loyalty? Our check stubs can reveal it.

BEWARE OF THE TYRANNY OF POSSESSIONS

Jesus warns us against putting our trust in riches or things that can erode. Do not invest your life in those things which can be stolen away. Seek to be free from the tyranny of things. Do not be dominated by those values which have no eternal dimensions to them. Too often our lives are tempted by those things which last only for the moment — money, possessions, power, houses, or fame. But they do not enable us to build any kind of lasting "wealth" that goes beyond them. They are all transient. Is our loyalty of heart to God or to "riches" which pass away? Paul warns us not to be tempted by material things that pull us away from our commitment to Christ. Jesus says "lay up your treasure in heaven." This was a phrase often identified with the "character" of persons. We are challenged to build the kind of inner character that can give us eternal significance. Our real loyalties need to be built on values that reach beyond earthly possessions as an end in themselves. Our heavenly commitment focuses on things other than just material possessions or earthly riches.

J. B. Priestly has a play entitled *They Came to the City*. A wealthy London man named Cudworth died. He goes to the place called "The City of Fulfilled Hopes." When he arrives there, people asked him what he did on earth. He replied: "I made money." And they asked: "Why?" He said, "To make more money." And they laughed at him. "To make money only as an end has no meaning here, no value." They believed that a person made money for some purpose beyond the acquiring of money. Money was a means only in life for some eternal significance. And to them Cudworth was a humorous specimen because he had wasted his time and possessed nothing. In the light of real values his life was indeed tragic.

AVOIDING SELF-CENTEREDNESS

Is that not what Paul is reminding young Timothy and us about the false allure of possessions? How easily we can be drawn into the temptations of the world that can lead us down destructive paths that carry us away from God. The love of money continuously looms before us as a road away from God and into selfishness and personal arrogance. Only a deep commitment to Christ and a constant desire to serve Him and follow His way can keep us from being drawn into the dead-end street of materialism.

An interesting book was published a couple of years ago entitled *New Rules*. In that book the author, Daniel Yankelovick, who is a social scientist, reports a tremendous shift in American values. In a study made from 1970 to 1980, he discovered that we have become the "meism" generation. Only twenty percent of adult Americans in our society today do not see as the first loyalty in their life to get something for self. Self-fulfillment is now the number one goal. Self-denial is no longer the first priority. To these folks, it no longer makes sense. What is harmful and harmless have replaced the old norm of right and wrong. Self is placed at the very center of life. The church needs to yell and proclaim as loudly as it can that this is sin. Those of us who claim to be Christians need to see if we walk down the road of "meism," in which our **basic** goal in life is simply to acquire possessions, earthly riches, or just to satisfy self, that we have not truly understood the teachings of Jesus Christ. Where your treasure is there will be your heart, and where your heart is there will be your treasure.

GIVING AS A PART OF WORSHIP

Giving is a part of our worship because it reflects where our commitment is. Our giving reveals whether or not our first loyalty is to God or to something of lesser value. We state in the bulletin each Sunday that we "worship through giving," because our giving is indeed a part of our worship. It reflects a deeper commitment of self to the Christ. It is an outward sign of an inward commitment. Through our giving there is acknowledged a holiness and wholeness about our lives. What I place in the offering plate reflects a deeper commitment which I have already made of myself to the Christ. My tithe and offerings show that I have a singleness of purpose in my life and that is to serve and follow Jesus Christ as the risen Lord. My giving is one way I show my support of His way.

When a hunter uses his gun he must use both sights on it. If a hunter is going to hit a target, he or she will have to get the two sights on the barrel lined up with each other. You have got to have the far sight and the near sights lined up or you will never hit a target. Too many people go through life and miss the real goal because they use only their near sight. They are not able to see the further dimension and get their goals and purpose lined up now so that they can have a heavenly glimpse of what is the purpose of living for earthly sake. Paul cautions us to aim our lives so we can develop "godliness" and live with an attitude of "contentment" with what we have materially.

COMMITMENT TO CHRIST COMES FIRST

Our focus in life needs to be on a goal that has ultimate significance and is not just of passing or temporary significance. Any genuine giving begins with the giving first of self. All true giving is a reflection of whether or not you and I have first committed ourselves to God. If I have not really given myself, then my giving is going to reflect that lack of a deeper commitment.

I heard of three small girls who wanted to surprise their mother with a birthday gift. The oldest of the girls brought a gift which she wrapped up and placed on a tray. She sang *Happy Birthday* to her mother and then gave her the gift. Another daughter came in with the same tray, and had a small dish on it. She sang *Happy Birthday*, and then gave the dish to the mother. The youngest girl had not been clued in by the others that she was supposed to buy something. But she was not dismayed. She walked into the room, put the tray on the floor, then, stood on the tray, and sang *Happy Birthday* to her mother. Then she flung herself into her mother's arms. Her gift was herself. Giving begins with the giving of self. Any kind of giving that we will have in our church is first a reflection that we have given our lives to Jesus Christ. Then, we are ready to follow Him as Lord and Master in our lives.

REASONS SOME DO NOT GIVE

Some of the reasons for our giving, or the lack of giving, reveals mixed motives and purposes. Some of you may have read or seen the letter that a pastor received several years ago. It reflects some of the reasons why people do not want to give. The letter reads:

> Dear Dr. Jones:
>
> In reply to your request to send a check, I wish to inform you that the present condition of my bank account makes it almost impossible. My shattered condition is due to the federal laws, the state laws, the county laws, corporation laws, mother-in-law, sister-in-law, and outlaws. Through these laws I am compelled to pay a business tax, amusement tax, head tax, school tax, gas tax, light tax, water tax, sales tax. Even my brain is taxed.
>
> I am required to get a business license, dog license, car license, truck license, not to mention a marriage license. I am also required to contribute to every organization which the genius of man is capable of bringing to life: woman's relief,

unemployment relief, every hospital and charitable institution in the city, including the Red Cross, the Black Cross, the Purple Cross, and the double cross. For my own safety, I am required to carry life insurance, property insurance, liability insurance, burglary insurance, accident insurance, business insurance, earthquake insurance, tornado insurance, unemployment insurance, old age insurance, and fire insurance. I am inspected, expected, disrespected, rejected, dejected, examined, re-examined, informed, reformed, summoned, fined, commanded and compelled until I provide an inexhaustible supply of money for every known need, desire, or hope of the human race. Simply because I refuse to donate something or other, I am boycotted, talked about, lied about, held up, held down, and robbed until I am ruined. I can tell you honestly that had not the unexpected happened, I could not enclose this check. The wolf that comes to so many doors nowadays just had pups in the kitchen. I sold them and here is the money.

OUR CHURCH'S PRESENT NEED

We all have excuses for giving or not giving. There is no question that this is true. Our church is now faced with a great challenge before us. Our church had this past year the best financial year we have ever had. This was accomplished under some very difficult circumstances. We gave the largest receipts our church has ever received to the *Together We Build* building program. At the same time, you gave well to our mission causes and the Cooperative Baptist Fellowship offering. But we are faced as a congregation with several challenges. Our Deacons are challenging each of you, knowing of your deep commitment to this church, to give sacrificially next Sunday to help eradicate these challenges. You will receive some special envelopes this week through the mail. With those envelopes we are asking you to do several things: First, to indicate a recommitment of your life to Christ; second, make a reaffirmation of your commitment to St. Matthews Baptist Church, and third, make a commitment of yourself to give to this special challenge offering to help meet this deficit need, and lastly, to increase your giving to our church.

Now I think that you can do that and will do that as a congregation. We have some of our people who have already pledged that they will give a thousand dollars to help meet this need. There are others who are going to give more. I hope that every family will give at least fifty dollars. We have a heavy burden upon us, and we must face it. But more than this immediate need is the long term over-all giving pattern of our congregation that we must change. We have some people who have given heroically to our church. Some of our people live on pensions, but they give very generously and faithfully to our church. I am proud of their sacrificial giving. Many of you are giving to the *Together We Build* program. I commend you for that. But we must give to our ongoing programs and ministries of this congregation as well. You are needed. Your giving is important. Each of us needs to consider his/her commitment and how essential it is for our church's ministry. I pray that our giving be a reflection of our deeper commitment to Jesus Christ as Lord.

Yesterday I talked to one of our Deacons who is retired. He said that he and his wife had tithed for years and now in his time of retirement, he works in his shop and the small amount of money he gets from that work, he gives fifty percent of that to his church. I hope that you and I will be challenged to see the kind of commitment which many of our people have. There is a great future ahead for this church. But you are needed. Your giving is needed. Each and every one of us needs to do his or her share of the giving. About a hundred families basically are carrying this church. The need is for all of us to be more deeply committed to serving Christ through our congregation.

GIVING THAT COSTS SOMETHING

In 2 Samuel we read the story about David in which he offers to purchase an animal to sacrifice and an altar on which he will make his sacrifice. A non-Jew, Araunah, offers to give King David both the animal for sacrifice and the threshing floor for a place for his altar. But David rejects Araunah's gift and purchased the site and sacrifices. Before David makes a sacrifice to God, he acknowledges his sin and accepts his responsibility for his sin. When David presents to God his sacrifice and worship, his gift represents his own self-denial. David says, "I will not offer worship to my God which cost me nothing." I hope that you and I will learn a lesson from David. Worship like grace is costly. The site which David purchased later became the place where the Temple was built. It marked a new beginning for David and Israel.

OUR TIME TO GIVE

May this time and place mark a beginning for you and me. May our worship, like David's, reflect a genuine form of self-denial. Our giving is a reflection of our deeper commitment to Jesus Christ as Lord. Let us not come into our church to worship and study and let somebody else bear the load, pay for the building; somebody else pay to heat the building; or somebody else pay for the literature. May we not let somebody else carry the entire financial and leadership load, then, we simply accept it. Let us offer unto the Lord our God worship which has cost us something also. Albert Schweitzer once said: "While money will not bring about the Kingdom of God, the Kingdom of God cannot be delivered without money." The Kingdom needs your money because your money is a reflection of where your heart is. I pray to God that each of us will show our commitment in our giving. Let the tithe be the place where we begin. This kind of commitment will enable us to be the kind of church that Christ is challenging us to be.

We shall soon have some wonderful facilities. We have many deeply committed people in this congregation who give heroically beyond their means. But there are some of you who have not yet felt the challenge of Christ in your giving, and I hope you will. Someone once complained to their minister that the church was always talking about money. "It's expensive business to belong to a church," he groaned. The minister said, "It should be. It costs the One who redeemed the Church everything."

The Church is built on the sacrifice of Jesus Christ our Lord. Because of His sacrifice, we sing "love so amazing, so divine. Demands my soul, my life, my all." In just a moment you and I are going to sing a hymn in which we say that we are willing to give "our silver and our gold and not a mite would I withhold." Do we really mean it? I pray to God that we shall learn that the best things in life are really not free. The grace of God, which comes to you and me out of the abundance of God's love, demands that you and I give first our lives to God, and, then, we link our material possessions to His higher way. Our ultimate values are not limited to material things. When our love of God is in the right place, all of our material possessions will be a reflection of a much deeper commitment to Jesus Christ as Lord. I pray to God that it may be true. Let it begin with you and with me.

O God, You have blessed us beyond what we deserve. Help us to learn to give You our best even at a cost. May our love be for You and not our material possessions. Amen.

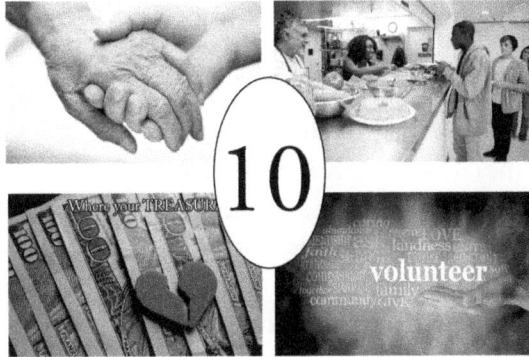

"How Much Are You Worth?"

Isaiah 39:1-8; Matthew 6:33-34

Several weeks ago newspapers and magazines reported who the richest persons in the United States were. Their net worth was listed. If you recall this story, the richest man in the United States at that time was the owner of Wal-Mart. He lives in Arkansas and is a multi-billionaire. Following the death of some persons, the newspaper often lists the net worth of an individual. It has always been interesting to me that the worth of a person is measured by what he had. Does that mean that the richest person in the United States is the individual who has the most money? Jesus did not measure human worth in that way. He used a different kind of measuring rod altogether. Let's see if we can discover what that is.

"Seek first the Kingdom of God," Jesus said, "and his righteousness, and all things will be given you" (Matthew 6:33). What is your most important quest in life? What is the treasure in your life? Is your primary search in life your financial holdings or real estate? Is it your stocks and bonds or your bank account? Is it fame or pleasure? What is your ultimate goal?

Several years ago a baseball game was underway with a very small umpire calling the pitches while standing behind a large catcher. A huge batter was at the plate. The call was one and one. The pitch came across the plate, and the umpire yelled, "Two."

Both the catcher and the batter turned around and asked: "Two what?"

"Too close to call," he answered.

When you look at the lives of some people, it is too close to call sometimes what their real purpose in their life is. They seem to have devoted their lives to the accumulation of things, possessions, and money. But they have lost something in that process. I have known rich people who have lost a loved one, exclaim that they would give all that they had to have that dead person back. Ask a parent who has lost a child or a husband or wife who has lost a mate if their material possessions can give them complete satisfaction for their loss. How many would give up all their possessions to have the person back whom they lost. I saw an inscription written on a tombstone once: "Here lies our most precious possession." An ancient inscription, written centuries ago declared: "Oh my life and Oh my love, Oh that I had died instead of you." We know that our possessions can never take the place of those we love.

What are you searching for and seeking in your life? Your "kingdom" is whatever you cannot do without. It is what you consider the most important thing in your life. Your "kingdom" is whatever you would be most miserable without. Your kingdom quest is what you would devote all of your time, effort, and total being to have. Your "kingdom" is whatever would give you the most unhappiness if you did not have it.

OUR PRIMARY GOAL

What is your ultimate quest in life? Obviously it should not just be your possessions. Jesus warned men and women centuries ago that their possessions might be lost or destroyed. In ancient times wealth was often measured by a person's fine clothing, gold or other precious possessions. Jesus warned that clothing could be destroyed by moths, and gold might be stolen. Thieves might break in a person's home and steal his gold. Today our possessions might be snatched away by depression, inflation, the falling of the market or robbery. "We can't take it with us" is a phrase we often use. We know that is true about physical things. They do not give us ultimate values in life, and yet again and again we measure our lives too often simply by what we have.

A minister was living next door to a lot where a new house was being constructed. He had watched the construction with interest. One day late in the afternoon he saw a pickup truck pull up in front of the lot. A man got out of the pickup truck and looked around to see if anybody was there. Not seeing anyone, he began to load some of the lumber on his pickup truck. The minister got his son's walkie-talkie and turned the volume up as loud as he could. He moved over as closely as he could to the man. He remained hidden behind some trees, and then in the deepest voice he had, he exclaimed: "Thou shall not steal." His voice came echoing across the lawn. The minister said that he knew the man was a Baptist, because he looked up. The man looked up and around to see where the voice came from. He did not see anyone, but then he quickly got in his truck and drove off.

God's voice comes to us in many quiet and subtle ways exclaiming, "Thou shall not steal." When you devote your life to the accumulation of things, you soon discover that who you are as a person is stolen away. Micah asked, "Will a man rob God?" Yet we consistently rob God again and again by devoting our lives to things. Too late we realize that our hearts and spirits have been stolen away, because our treasure is things.

THE SPIRITUAL HEART

Jesus said, "Where your treasure is there will be your heart also." What is your heart? Is the heart merely the physical organ for which our city has gained national recognition for its transplants? The biblical view of the heart does not limit it to the physical part of our anatomy. The Scriptures declare, "Out of the heart come the issues of life." Another writer prays, "Create within me a clean heart, O God." In another place the Scriptures state, "As a man thinks in his heart so he is." The heart was considered in the ancient biblical tradition to be the center of one's life. The heart is the center of one's personality. Out of it is expressed a person's will, thought, and love. It constitutes what is the authentic you as a person. Where your treasure is there you will find the real you. You will devote yourself to whatever you have placed first in your heart. What you have put first becomes the paramount thing in your life. Unfortunately, too many of us have devoted our lives to the pursuit of material ends. Our lives have taken a detour, and our hearts have gone down the wrong avenue. We have found ourselves in the land of famine in the midst of plenty. Sometimes our greediness for material things has taken us down dead-end streets that have consumed our very being. We have lost the purpose for which we were created.

SETTING SPIRITUAL PRIORITIES

Jesus did not tell all of His disciples that they had to forsake everything to follow Him. But He did tell us to set priorities in our life. All the material things we have are to be committed to spiritual ends. In Henry Van Dyke's story, *The Mansions*, he writes about a rich man who lived in a large mansion here on earth, but in heaven he had a tiny hut. He had not sent up any materials to build anything better. But a very poor doctor, who had devoted his life to working in a poverty section of the city and lived in a modest house, found that he had a great mansion in heaven. The point of this story is that in investing our lives here in the spiritual use of the gifts we have, we are investing in the life beyond this one in heaven. This is an investment which is secure. It cannot be snatched away from us. We need more people to make this kind of investment.

I was told recently about a couple in our church who matched their food budget, including meals they eat at home or when they go out, with an equal amount to be given to World Hunger. They have determined that this is one way they can make everything they do have some spiritual consequences. Most of us give little reflection to the spiritual significance of our possessions. Jesus has challenged us to use our material resources for spiritual ends. Our material possessions are our servants not our masters. "Where your treasure is," Jesus said, "there will be your heart."

The greatest challenge Jesus has given us is to "seek first the Kingdom of God." If we are honest, we will have to say that even those of us who claim to be Christian do not really seek the Kingdom of God first, do we? Unfortunately, we seek primarily what we can have in the moment.

WHEN WE ARE CONCERNED ONLY ABOUT TODAY

At this point, Hezekiah steps on the scene. The ancient king, Hezekiah, had reigned in Jerusalem for twenty-eight years. He had been a good king. He had brought peace to the land and removed idolatry from his nation. He walked in the company of Isaiah, Micah and Hosea. During this time, Hezekiah became seriously ill. He thought he was going to die and prayed to God: "O God, if you will make me well, I will do thus and so for you." While he was ill, he made all kinds of commitments to God. Later when he got well, like so many, he forgot his prayer. Some Babylonian leaders heard of his illness, and came, they said, to rejoice with him in his restored health. Unfortunately, Hezekiah brought these officials into his palace and showed them all that he had. He showed them his possessions and military strength. They asked him to make an alliance with them against Assyria.

The prophet Isaiah, after seeing the dignitaries from Babylon leave, asked the king what this meeting meant. The king told him what he had done. Then Isaiah said to him, "Hear now the word from the Lord. Your children will be taken in captivity to Babylon. This city will be devastated and nothing will be left." Listen to the amazing response of Hezekiah: "The word of the Lord is good." Good? In what way? Good in the sense that he would have a peaceful reign. He would not personally face any suffering and difficulties. His children would be the ones to bear that load and not him.

Hezekiah still walks among us, doesn't he? He does not worry about tomorrow. He is concerned only with the present moment. He will not do anything to make the burden lighter for his children so they will be safe and secure for the future. How absurd can this be?

Our church is saying very loudly and clearly that you are needed today. Your support is needed in the *Together We Share* program, and in the regular financial load which your church bears all the time. If you are waiting for somebody else to bear this financial load tomorrow, there will be no tomorrow for our church. Each one of us must carry his or her part of the load today. Your church is giving you a clear opportunity to direct your material resources for higher goals. Be careful that material ends do not become the dominant force in your life. Everywhere we turn we are bombarded with the view that material things make life complete. From the very beginning of his or her life, a small child likes to receive more than to give. A child has to be taught to give, and so must we. All of us need to remember the danger of the legendary Midas who turned everything he touched to gold. At first it seemed great, but soon he realized the danger of his touch. Gold and other possessions cannot give us lasting satisfaction. Our possessions cannot love us back, cannot give us friendship, and cannot give us happiness in themselves. Things have meaning only as they are used for some cause beyond themselves. They are not ends in themselves. Set priorities in your life to use your material possessions in God's service.

Our Challenge to Give

Recently I examined some statistics about giving in our church. Some of the people who are counted in these statistics probably do not attend church, but some of you do. This means that some of our congregation, who may have large incomes, give less to their church than they might spend on the popcorn they would eat at movie theatres in a year's time. Some of our members who are on Social Security are among our finest givers. Many of these persons tithe and do the best that they can on a small income. Forty-three percent of our people also indicated that they should be giving more to our church. This is the moment. This is it. Not later. NOW. This is when your church needs you. Eighteen percent of our people said that they realize they need to start tithing. This is that moment. Start giving to your church. This is the time of need. For some people to give a hundred dollars a year to our church is a real sacrifice. Their income is low. But for some others who receive large salaries that same gift is embarrassingly small. What a person gives indicates something about his or her commitment to Christ and His church.

I read about a church that was having a building fund drive. As they were counting the pledge cards, the counting committee came across one from a woman in the congregation who pledged three hundred and ninety dollars over a period of three years. They looked at her pledge and decided to visit her, because they thought it was too large. They knew that the sole source of her income came from the washing that she took in three days a week. When they spoke to her about reducing her pledge, she told them about her plan. She received three dollars for each washing and she had been washing three days a week. She was going to take in washing one more day a week and that day she would be working for the Lord and dedicate her earnings to her church. One day a week she would wash for her church.

We need that kind of sacrifices. We need persons who are willing to make a commitment to the church of Christ and do their part. Some of our members do everything they can to support our church financially. Recently I visited a church member whose husband was very ill in the hospital. On two different occasions this individual gave me her offering envelope to put in the offering plate. Although she could not come to church, she wanted her tithe to get to church. Recently a woman sat in my study and told me that she was putting her church in her will. She wanted a portion of her money to be used by this congregation after her death in a way to bless the lives of others. You will never convince me, and you cannot convince yourself, that you have put the kingdom of God first in your life when your money does not reflect it.

"Seek first the kingdom of God," Jesus told His followers. That doesn't mean you have to give all you have to God and the church. But Christ has instructed you to dedicate all of your life, including your money, to Him.

You and I sanctify the whole of our possessions by giving a part of our money to God and His church. We can't always be receivers only. We must decide to be givers. Emily and I have given a tithe to our church since we have been married. We have made a commitment to give to the *Together We Share* program above our tithe. This is more than double what we have given, and I challenge you to do the same. If you make thirty, forty, fifty, or seventy thousand dollars, you cannot expect your church to pay off the *Together We Share* debt when you make a pledge of only fifty or a hundred dollars. Some of you need to make a pledge of ten thousand dollars. Some of you can give twenty thousand, fifty thousand or more. But every one of you needs to make some kind of sacrificial gift to this church. If you are going to seek first God's kingdom, you need to take your giving seriously.

Paul, writing to the Corinthian church, told them: "You have been bought with a price." God gave His son. He laid down His life on the cross for you and me. We have been bought by His sacrificial love. Surely ... SURELY we can be willing to make commitments to Him to show our gratitude for His love.

A president, who was speaking at a state university graduating service, said to the students: "Much of your education has been paid for by the state. I hope you are going to be worth what you cost." Do you ever have the feeling that God may ask that question of us? He has given all for us. Are you and I worth what we have cost Him? I pray that our commitment will show that we are.

O Loving God, You have given so much for us. May we be willing to give much back to You. Through Christ, who gave His all for us, we pray. Amen.

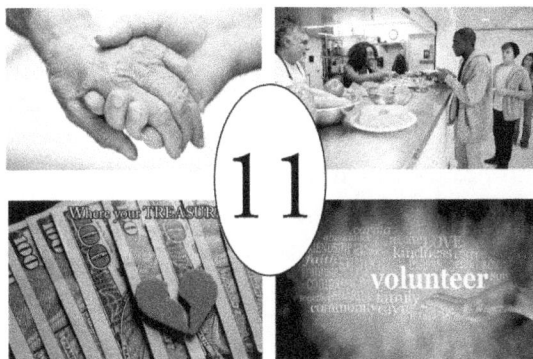

"WHAT'S IN IT FOR ME?"

Acts 3:1-10

A beggar routinely went to the Temple each day in ancient Jerusalem. After all, he had been going there for many years. He had been lame since birth, and at forty years old, he had begged either at this place or some other spot all of his life. He didn't come to the Temple with any great expectations, but he did hope that somebody would notice him that day and give him some small alms. He sat outside the Temple gate at the mid-afternoon time of prayer. He saw two strangers walking toward him. As he saw these men approaching him, he may have hoped that these two might give him some small contribution. So he began to beg more loudly. Peter and John walked up and stopped in front of the man. The beggar must have continued to beg from others who passed by, because Peter called out to the beggar: "Look at us!"

The beggar turned and looked up at them with anticipation and hope that he would receive something from them. "Silver and gold have I none," Peter said, "but what I have I give to you. In the name of Jesus of Nazareth, rise and walk." He reached over, took the man by his hand and pulled him up. The beggar discovered that his feet and ankle bones were healed. The words used here to describe his feet and ankle bones are technical medical phrases which are not used any place else in the New Testament. He walked with Peter and John into the Temple, and then he began to leap and praise God. The crowd marveled at the miracle which they had seen.

Now this is a fantastic story. It is the first miracle by any of the disciples after the death of Jesus and following Pentecost which was recorded in the Book of Acts. Look at the lame beggar. He had sat at the Temple gate for years. What a contrast this man in his helplessness was with the strength and beauty which surrounded him at the Temple. He sat there daily hoping and wishing for some help. But for years nothing had happened in his life to improve his condition or circumstances.

WHO IS THE BEGGAR TODAY?

Who does that beggar represent to you? Who is the beggar that sits at the church's gate today? There are many persons who sit at the gates of the churches today who suffer from cancer, heart trouble, Alzheimer's disease, and other illnesses who are waiting for someone to reach out to minister to them in the name of Christ. Who does this paralyzed beggar represent to you? Does he represent those who are paralyzed by their sins and unable to find freedom from them, because they are caught in bad habits, routines and wiles that have led them down dead-end streets? Does this man at the gate represent those who are paralyzed by their loneliness, depression, anxieties or fears? Whoever these people are who sit at the gate today, Jesus Christ is sending you and me, who claim to be His disciples, to reach out and minister to them.

Scholars have debated the location and description of the Gate Beautiful. Some are not sure whether it represents the Shushan Gate which was on the east side of the Temple area or the Nicanor Gate on the east side of the Temple proper. Some scholars have identified the Beautiful Gate with the Corinthian Gate. Josephus describes the Corinthian Gate in much detail. It was made of bronze and adorned with silver and gold. An image of a vine was on the door symbolizing the nation of Israel. The doors were forty cubits high (60 to 70 feet). This gate led from the Court of the Gentiles into the Court of the Women. The lame man may have sat outside these doors each day.

Studies of Herod's Temple which are based on the works of Josephus and others indicate that there were at least eight gates to the Temple. The Beautiful Gate or the Golden Gate faced the Mount of Olives. Four gates were located on the opposite west side from the Beautiful Gate. Two opened to the south and one to the north. Several of these gates opened outward to the city of Jerusalem, one to the king's palace and others toward the suburbs and the outer community.[1] Sometimes the temple/church has directed more energy in walking down the road toward the seat of government than the other pathway. Too often it has tried to bind itself with government rather than reaching out to the hurting world down the other streets.

Jesus told a powerful parable recorded in the sixteenth chapter of Luke's gospel. It begins with the nineteenth verse and reads: "There was once a rich man, who dressed in purple and the finest linen, and feasted in great magnificence every day. At his gate, covered with sores, lay a poor man named Lazarus, who would have been glad to satisfy his hunger with the scraps from the rich man's table." (The whole parable is found in Luke 16:19-31.)

THE BEGGAR NOW SITS AT THE CHURCH'S GATE

The beggar sits at the church's gate, and no longer can the Church say with Peter, "Silver and gold have I none." *The Church* has unlimited financial resources. The beggar sits at our gate in his agony, awaiting you, me, and others to reach out to him or her and help them. You and I are challenged by Christ to reach out to these people. But often we do not want to see their faces. We turn off the television sets and cast the magazines and newspapers aside. We don't want to look at gaunt faces, swollen stomachs, protruding eyes, and begging hands from countries of the world or our own inner cities where people are hungry, live on the streets, are without work, and extend their hands for help to us. They make us uncomfortable. We had rather ignore the beggars at our gates, in

---

1 See the article on the "Jerusalem Temple" in *The Interpreter's Dictionary of the Bible*, R-Z Vol. (Nashville: Abingdon Press, 1962), 534-560.

our cities, and around the world. We avoid looking at or hearing the cries of the Lazaruses of the world. We leave them begging at the gates and pretend they do not exist. And for many of us, as far as meeting their needs, we ignore them completely.

A mother, sister, and young boy were sitting at a lunch counter. After the mother and sister had ordered, the waitress turned to the young boy and asked him what he wanted. The sister replied, "I'll order for him."

The waitress asked the young man again: "What would you like, son?"

The mother said, "I'll order for him."

Ignoring these comments, the waitress turned to the boy again and asked: "Young man, what would you like?"

"I'd like a hamburger," he said.

"How would you like it fixed? Medium, rare, or well done?"

"Well done," he replied.

"Would you like it with mustard, pickle, ketchup, onions or relish?"

"I'll take the works," he said.

As the waitress walked away, the little boy observed: "Gee, Mommy, she thinks I'm real!"

Too many people do not think that the begging, hurting people of the world are real. "It is their fault they are like they are," some cry. But some people are born in countries where they will never have a decent meal in their whole lifetime. With all of the wealth, abundance, and splendor in our country, we ignore the beggars at our gate and do nothing. Do you ever wonder about the judgment of God? Remember that Jesus pronounced harsh judgment on those who were unwilling to give a cup of water, feed the hungry, or visit those in prison when they saw the need. What would he say to us today?

AN EXPECTANT LOOK

"Look at us," Peter said to the lame man. The beggar looked up hopefully and expectantly. Then Peter said, "Silver and gold we don't have." Oh, how his heart must have sunk. He had looked up in expectation that these two strangers would give him some alms so he would not have to go home empty-handed again. "Look at us." "Focus your attention on us. Quit looking at everybody else walking by. You may miss something."

Then Peter said, "What I have, I give you." The man had asked for silver and gold, but Peter gave him something else. He did not give him what he had asked for, but he gave him something more significant. Thank goodness God does not always give us what we ask for. We think we know what we always need. But graciously God often does not give us just what we ask.

The beggar also could not buy what he needed. Even if he had had great wealth, he could not buy what Peter wanted to give him. Do you remember the story about Simon the Magician who tried to buy the healing power of Peter? Peter said to him: "Your money perish with you, because you thought you could obtain the gift of God with your money!" (Acts 8:9-24). The beggar could not buy what Peter had to give him.

WHAT I HAVE I GIVE

But Peter said, "What I have I give to you." He could give, because the gospel of Jesus Christ — the good news — the healing power, is for sharing. The grace Peter had received was not for keeping, hoarding, possessing, but for giving. If you hug love to yourself, you lose it. Love stays alive by reaching out and hugging somebody else. If you try to keep joy to yourself, it disappears. Real joy cries out to be shared with others. The Christian faith is not to be kept selfishly for ourselves. It is something that, if we have it, we will share it. We will want to let others know about and share in what we have experienced in Jesus Christ.

WHAT'S IN IT FOR ME ATTITUDE

Boy, that really cuts against the grain of today's world, doesn't it? The beggar sat by the Temple gate trying to see what he could get from those who passed by. Many today live with the philosophy which the beggar had as he sat by the gate. "What's in it for me?" "What can I get today?" This philosophy focuses on what can I get from others? Its only concern seems to be: "What can a particular person or this institution do for me? I'll scratch your back, if you will scratch mine." This is reflected in the desire of the man who told me recently that he wanted to see if I could set up a luncheon engagement for him with a particular person, because he wanted to see if he could get him to do something for him. "He has connections you know," he said to me. Look at the titles of some popular books today: *The Psychology of Winning, Looking Out for # One, Think and Grow Rich, The Master Key to Riches,* and *Grow Rich with Peace of Mind.*

Many are only looking out for number one. They are like the farmer in one of the parables of Jesus who was concerned with building greater barns. His emphasis was on "my" barns, "my" riches, and "I." "I" echoes throughout the parable. Selfishness was the primary focus. It is sad when a person's primary concern is: "What's in it for me?" Some people even look for a church with the attitude: "What's in it for me? What can the church do for me, my children, and my family?" This is not to say that we should have no concern about these areas. But have you asked yourself the question: "What can **I** do for my church in service and ministry?"

Several years ago, a ninety-four-year-old woman died in Chicago. In her old, rambling house, the administrator of her estate found priceless antiques of every description and size packed into twenty rooms. Some of the rooms were so crowded with fine china and other antiques that one could not walk through the room. When the false bottom of an old trunk was removed, a fortune in diamonds was discovered. Five thousand dollars in cash was found in a desk along with un-cashed checks which were now worthless.

Money orders which had been there for decades had to be sent to Washington to be redeemed. This woman had wealth beyond her imagination, and all she did with it was hoard it. She never used it. Is that a proper use of our possessions?

A communist wrote these lines a few years ago. "I give all of my time to the party, and well over fifty percent of my money. No wonder Christianity is so weak, for you are proud when you give a few hours of one day occasionally, and you gloat with the gift of a few dollars to your cause every few weeks. I don't believe you when you say that the Christian faith is so great — for how could you give so little if it were?"

OUR GIVING SHOULD REFLECT OUR BLESSINGS

Peter said, "What I have I give to you." You and I have experienced so many blessings from God. Our giving should reflect our appreciation for these blessings. Each year our church sets up a budget to carry out our ministry for Christ. Our budget establishes goals and limits for doing our various church programs, ministries and mission work here and around the world. Without your support of this regular budget, we cannot conduct our daily, weekly, monthly, and annual ministries. This year our pledge card will have two boxes — one for our regular budget and another for our Building Enhancement. Your commitment to both of these is essential. Your pledge to the building is important, but you need to be faithful in your continued support of our regular budget as well. Our stewardship commitment is a reflection of our deeper commitment to our Lord. The support of all of our members is necessary. If we really are committed to our Lord, then we will give faithfully.

A visitor to our services recently sent me a short story from a Zen Buddhist collection. The story is about a merchant of Edo named Umezu Seibei who gave five hundred pieces of gold called *ryo* to Seisetsu, who was the master of Engaku in Kamakura. He gave the gold so the school could be expanded. The teacher, Seisetsu, said, "All right, I will take it." But Umezu was not very pleased with the attitude of the teacher. He noted that one could live for a whole year on three *ryo*, and he had not been thanked for a sack of five hundred! "You told me that before," observed Seisetsu.

"Even if I am a wealthy merchant, five hundred ryo," Umezu said, "is a lot of money."

"Do you want me to thank you for it?" asked the teacher.

"You ought to," replied Umezu.

"Why should I?" asked Seisetsu. "The giver should be thankful!"[1]

You and I, who receive so much, should be thankful that we have opportunities to give and the resources with which we can give. Instead of being thanked for giving, we need to rejoice that we can give. Like Peter, what we have, we give.

THE IMPORTANCE OF REACHING OUT TO THOSE IN NEED

Then Peter reached out and touched the beggar. He took him by the hand with a strong grip and pulled him to his feet. He touched him. The church must continue to reach out to the lame, the beggars, the hurting of the world, and touch them. It is not enough just to think about them, study about them, or even pray about them. But we are challenged to reach out, like our Lord did, and touch them. If we do not, we will leave the lame man in his paralysis, the beggar at the gate, the woman at the well, and the blind man in his darkness. Jesus Christ has called His followers to reach out and touch those who are in need. I am convinced that there are basically two kinds of people in life. There are those who are the by-standers and those who stand by. The bystanders always just watch what is happening but do not do anything. But those who stand by get involved and minister to those in need. The Priest and Levi in the Parable of the Good Samaritan represent those who were only bystanders. They walked by on the other side. The Good Samaritan represents the one who was willing to stand by and give assistance. Peter was not merely a bystander. He was one who stood

---

1   Paul Reps, *Zen Flesh, Zen Bones* (New York: Doubleday Co., 1961), 48.

by. He reached out and helped this beggar. We are challenged by our Lord to stand by and reach out and touch the needy.

THE POWER TO BLESS COMES FROM CHRIST

But note that Peter performed this miracle "In the name of Jesus Christ of Nazareth." Isn't that fantastic? Just a few days before, Peter had denied that he even knew Jesus Christ. He denied Him three times in the courtyard after Jesus had been arrested. What made the difference in Peter's attitude? The resurrection of Jesus! Now he stands in the Temple and proclaims the name of Jesus like he was waving a banner for all to see. "In the name of Jesus of Nazareth, rise and walk." He knew the power for this healing was not in himself. He acknowledged that the power came from his Lord. He remembered that his Lord had promised that "Greater works than these (referring to his miracles) will he do, because I go to the Father" (John 14:12). With this assurance, Peter reached out to meet human needs.

BEGGING TRANSFORMED TO PRAISE

After the man was healed, he began to praise God. One moment he was begging and the next he was praising. He stood to his feet, walked, and then began to leap. When does your begging change to praising? Too often our worship seems to be more about begging God instead of praising Him.

An image of prayer as begging is depicted vividly in Maxwell Anderson's play, *High Tor*. Two men found themselves in grave danger, and they didn't know what to do. "Say, do you know any prayers?" Biggs asks.

Skimmerhorn says, "I know one."

"Say it, will you?" Biggs urges.

Skimmerhorn prays: "Matthew, Mark, Luke, and John, Bless the bed that I lie on."

"That's not much good, that one," Biggs responds.

But Skimmerhorn says, "It's the only one I know."

Suddenly there is a loud crash. As danger seems more imminent, Skimmerhorn cries, "I don't know how to pray."

Another crash. Biggs falls on his knees, "Oh, God I never did this before and I don't know how, but keep us safe here and I'll be a better man. I'll put candles on the altar, yes I'll get that Spring Valley Church fixed up, the one that's falling down. I can do a lot for You if You will let me live. Oh, God!"[1]

When we find ourselves between a rock and a hard place, then we begin to beg God, like the two in this play; many turn to God only in times of difficulty or emergency. Prayer for them is used like the fire alarm in public buildings. It is something to be used only "in case of emergency." When prayer is genuine, it has moved from the level of begging to praising. The psalmist calls us to praise again and again. "Praise the Lord! O give thanks to the Lord, for he is good, for his steadfast love endures forever! (Psalm 106:1). When does our begging change to praising? A beggar experienced the power of God, and he went away praising God.

WHAT HAPPENED TO THE BEGGAR?

Have you ever wondered what happened to that beggar? This miracle provoked Peter's great sermon which is recorded in Acts. But what happened to the beggar? Did he become a faithful follower of Jesus Christ and go with Peter, John, and the other disciples to share with others what God had done for him? He had received so much. Did he now give much in service? We don't know, do we? But we do know this. You …You … You … claim that once you were in sin, and Jesus Christ has given you redemption and made you whole. You have found wholeness — redemption. What are you doing for Jesus Christ today? Are you praising, giving, and serving God? We do not know the beggar's story, but yours and mine is being written now. What does it say?

O Father, having received so much, make us faithful in our giving and living. Through Christ, who gave His life that we might have life. Amen.

---

1   Maxwell Anderson, *High Tor* (New York: Anderson House, 1937, First Edition) Act One, Scene Three, 69.

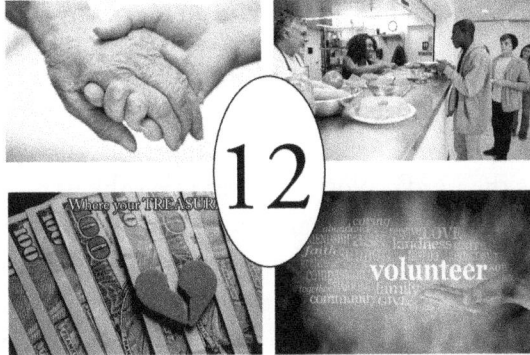

"SPIRITUAL AND MATERIAL RELIGION"

Psalm 24:1-10; Mathew 6:19-24

Years ago, when I was a child, I used to watch old Western movies built around the theme of claim jumpers. Miners would make a big discovery and rush to the claim office and try to stake their claim before somebody else could beat them to it. Sometimes a claim jumper would rush to the claim office ahead of the real owner and try to take over somebody else's claim. I always knew what would happen. There would be a big shoot-out at the end of the movie. Since Adam and Eve, there have been a lot of claim jumpers in the world. The socialists claim that the earth belongs to the state. The communists say it belongs to the workers. The capitalists say that it belongs to those who have the initiative to acquire and preserve it. But they are really wrong. The earth is the Lord's. We do not own any of it. We are only stewards of the earth.

That message seems to be belied on almost every hand today. Tractor trailer trucks roll down the highway with the name of its owner printed on its side. Retail stores flash with the name of its individual firm. Everywhere we look we see all kinds of indications that somebody else owns the earth. But we do not understand the reality of creation if we see ourselves as masters of the earth. The psalmist asserts that the earth is the Lord's, and we are only stewards of it. God has given His created world to us as a gift, and we can use and develop it. But we do not own it nor possess it.

SPIRITUALIZE THE MATERIAL

I want us to begin by reflecting on the necessity of spiritualizing the material. The psalmist reminds us that the earth is the Lord's — all of it — not just what happens in the sanctuary. But the earth is the Lord's. Notice the verb that the psalmist uses. It is not *was*, or *will be*, but the earth **is** the Lord's — all of it.

In the ancient Greek thinking, the body was seen as evil. They believed that one should escape the flesh. But the Jewish Christian tradition has always taught that the body is good. It was created by God, and the body is the temple of the Holy Spirit where God continues to rule and reign. The world which God created is called a universe — not a multi-verse. It is a universe, united by God who created His world with cohesiveness, oneness, and inter-relatedness. At the center of the universe is a spiritual force — God's presence. God's power unifies all of creation and life. God created a universe. Too often we try to divide life into the sacred and the secular, and the two are never supposed to meet. What a person does in church does not touch his or her life outside church. Religion is one thing, but the work-a-day world is seen as something else altogether. Jesus never made that kind of division between the sacred and secular. They are intertwined. What one does in his or her work and the rest of life is a reflection of one's religion.

Back in the fourth and fifth centuries, there was a man named Simeon Stylites who for thirty years lived on a platform thirty feet off the ground. People sent his food and every necessity up to him. For thirty years, he never came down from that platform. He was separating himself from the world, seeking to follow the injunction of Jesus "to be separate from the world." But that was not the kind of separation for which Jesus was calling. That's foolishness. To separate one's self from the world like that prevents us from being the salt, the light, or the leaven. We are to be separated from evil, but the Christian is called to be the transforming, redemptive force to change society.

Notice what Jesus said about ownership. In the Scripture passage from Matthew's gospel, Jesus spoke about persons who wanted to own clothes as a sign of valuable possessions. But Jesus warned that moths might easily destroy the wealth tied up in clothes. Others thought that they could have great possessions by putting their money in grain. The word "rust" is really better translated "eaten away." Mice or rats might enter a granary and destroy the grain. Others put their trust for security in gold. Unfortunately, gold could be easily stolen. Many ancient houses were made of mud, and one could simply knock a hole through the wall or dig through it and steal somebody's gold. Jesus said: "Do not put your ultimate trust in clothes that will wear out, in possessions that can be eroded away, or in money that can be stolen. Put your trust in something that will last — something that has eternal significance." The Scriptures do not say that money is the root of all evil. It says that "**the love of money** is the root of all evil."

Money can be used for spiritual ends. It can be spiritualized and used in God's Kingdom. When we begin to see that the earth is the Lord's and everything that we have belongs to Him, then we realize that all we have can be used in ways to further His Kingdom. We have to learn, first of all, to spiritualize the material. This means that everything we have — our houses, lands, automobiles, bank accounts - all belong to the Lord, and we are simply stewards of it. We use what God has given us. We spiritualize the material when we use the material for spiritual ends. The way we use our possessions testifies to the deeper values in our lives.

In his book, *A Diary of Private Prayer*, John Baillie has voiced a prayer to God that we all should pray: "Let me always keep in mind that the things that matter are not money or possessions, not houses or property, not bodily comforts or pleasures, but truth and honor and gentleness and helpfulness and a pure love of you."[1] Let's try daily to make that your prayer and my prayer.

---

1   John Baillie, *A Diary of Private Prayer*, updated and revised by Susanna Wright (New York: Scribner, 2014), 47.

MATERIALIZE THE SPIRITUAL

Secondly, we have got to materialize the spiritual. There are some "holy folks" who just love to talk about how spiritual they are. They claim that they are more spiritual than we are because of the way they pray, or because they have received a "special blessing" or something else. But the sad thing is that their spirituality is often in some lofty, high ideals. It never touches life. You can't get a handle on it. In fact, you can't even see it in their lives. What they say is not reflected in what they do. They talk about religion, but they do not live it. They sometimes even pray about religion, but their lives do not reflect it in any way. Religion is some lofty ideal. Church to them is cloudy and vague but never takes on reality. Church is always more than place, but it is a place. Church doesn't just exist as an idea. Jesus established His church as a living, functioning organism. Religion, if it is real, has always got to have a material reflection.

A PROCESSIONAL HYMN

Psalm 24 is called a processional psalm.[1] Pilgrims were traveling to Jerusalem to worship God in their holy Temple. As they approached the city gates, they cried out: "Lift up the gates." Response came from the priest inside or a chorus who asked the pilgrims: "Who can ascend to the hill of the Lord?" The response came from another choir or priest who declared: "Those who have clean hands and pure hearts." Do you hear it? Religion is reflected in material life. It is not enough just to come inside the temple. Those who came to worship in the temple were expected to let their religion be seen in their living, in their relationships with one another, and in their business dealings. This was symbolized in their clean hands. Micah has reminded worshipers: "What does the Lord require of you but to do justice, to love mercy, and to walk humbly with your God?" Those who claim that religion takes place only

---

1   J. Clinton McCann, Jr., *The Book of Psalms: The New Interpreter's Bible* (Nashville: Abingdon Press, 1996), 772.

inside of church buildings have never understood the message of the Bible. Religion touches all of life.

This was illustrated for me superbly a number of years ago when I came across a *Peanut's* comic strip. Snoopy is sitting in the snow shivering. Charlie Brown and Linus see him in that sad condition. "You know, we should do something about that," Linus says. "He looks cold and hungry. Let's go over and help him." So he walks over and pats him on the head and says, "Be warmed, be fed, be comforted." Then he walks off and leaves him shivering in the cold.

That story is straight out of the New Testament where James declares that faith without works is dead. It is easy to talk about how much I love God, how I love religion, or even to sing pious songs, chant pious prayers, or preach lofty sermons. We can sit and look so pious, but if our religion doesn't touch our living, it is nonsense and not real at all. Faith without works is dead.

GOD CREATED THE MATERIAL WORLD

God was not ashamed of the material world. God created it from nothing. God created material things, including man and woman, and said of all His creation: "It is good" — not perfect — but good. When God became incarnate, God came into the world in the flesh. God entered the world as a human being and dwelt among us. William Temple, a noted English theologian, once said that Christianity is "the most avowedly materialistic of all the great religions." Why would a theologian make such a claim? Because God created the material world. Because the Word became flesh. God did not view flesh or the world as evil nor did He see material things as evil. The material is a means of grace. Jesus was often seen eating in the homes of wealthy persons. But what did He do when He was there? He challenged them to use their wealth for higher spiritual needs, never to make money as an end in itself.

Why should we want to help other people? The answer is simply to get outside of our own selfishness, to break free from always putting one's self at the center of life, to aim for a higher goal in life, to let God rule our life so that we can use our possessions for a cause greater and more lasting than ourselves.

This past week I received a letter from a couple who are not members of our church. They started coming to our church after first hearing our program on the radio. Then, they started coming to worship. In the letter, the writer indicated how much they liked the worship service, the sermons, the music, and the magnificent place we have in which to worship. The couple sent a check for three hundred dollars. Although they are not members of our church or denomination, they have come to our church and have found meaning and inspiration in worship. They decided not merely to be receivers but givers.

Our church is facing the greatest challenge it has had since the fire. Our budget is $1,132,813, plus whatever we give to our mission causes. If that doesn't scare you, you haven't looked at it very carefully. It ought to. It is frightening when we think of the money we must raise. It is 14% above what we gave last year, including our regular budget and the *Together We Build* gifts. Our Stewardship Committee is saying to each of us that we can do it, but it will be challenging. It means that every single one of us must do his or her part in giving to the regular budget. Those who have been giving to TWB must continue to give their gifts by now giving to the Sanctuary Debt Retirement. New members, who have not been giving to the TWB are now challenged to give to the Sanctuary Debt Retirement as well as the regular offering. We don't know what our final receipts will be for this year, but our offerings are a bit above last year, so we are hoping that we will not have a difference of 14% this year.

Yes, it is a challenging budget. But it would not be a challenge at all if every single one of us tithed. Instead of leaving it up to a few to carry the whole load, if each of us shared the load, it would be much easier to bear. Some of us will sit in this magnificent place of worship and not share the obligation to support its ministry. I give because our church has opportunities to minister in marvelous ways in this community. We have a magnificent place to worship. We have a splendid ministry of music and fine Sunday School, youth, and children's programs. Through our Grandview Educational Association, we have a Counseling Center, a Kindergarten, a Mother's Day Out program, a Job Club, an Alzheimer's Day Care Center, and a multitude of other kinds of programs. There are so many ways that our church serves in our community, city, and beyond. It is a marvelous challenge that we have before us. I hope you will try to help us meet it. I tithe because it is a part of my worship of God. I tithe because it is my acknowledgement that God is the owner of my life, that the earth is the Lord's. I tithe because it is a part of my responsibility to carry on the ministry of the Church here and around the world.

Years ago when highwaymen would attempt to rob someone, they would cry: "Your money or your life." Everyone, of course, would give up his money rather than his life. Jesus said, "I have come that you might have life" — not money. Money is a way of serving Him in all that we do and have. Money is not the end goal of our living, but a means of enabling us to share the "life" which we have found in God.

Years ago an officer challenged his soldiers to go on a very dangerous mission. "I could appoint three men to go on this mission," he said, "but I would like three volunteers. I'm going to turn my back," he declared, "and see if three volunteers will step forward." He turned his back and waited a moment, then, when he turned around he could not see any difference in the troops. No one seemed to step forward. He looked rather irritated and was about to speak when his sergeant spoke up and said: "But, sir, the whole battalion has stepped forward — all of us have stepped forward."

We have a great challenge before us. I hope that every single one of you will step forward and do your part and bear the stewardship responsibility of our church. The earth is the Lord's and all that we have belongs to Him. Let us be faithful in our stewardship. It is time for each of us to step forward.

O God of Mercy, we thank You for the challenge that is before us. May we measure up to it as we commit ourselves anew to You. Amen.

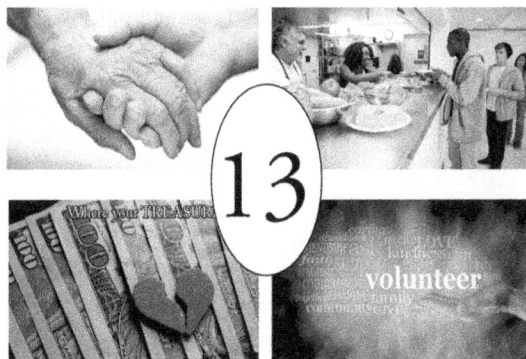

"Oh, I Don't Have Time or Money"

Matthew 25:1-30

When you have been in ministry as long as I have, I suppose one hears all kinds of excuses for not being active in church. When an individual is asked to do some service for his or her church, that individual may reply: "Well, I really don't have time to do it, but I'll drop an extra five dollars in the offering plate." Or, "I'll give a little bit of money." I recall vividly an encounter I had with an irate individual after I had preached a stewardship sermon in another congregation. He indicated to me that he did not believe in stewardship, and that instead of giving his money, he was going to give time. I can assure you that I watched very carefully to see how much *time* that individual gave to his church. I observed that he seldom gave any time to church causes, except occasionally coming to worship. I suppose one of the saddest excuses we hear from individuals, even if they do not verbalize it, but express it in non-verbal ways is: "Oh, I don't have time or money!"

Well, I would ask you if you have neither time nor money to give to your church and your God, then what in heaven's name *are* you going to give God? What else do you have? Time is the vehicle through which we express our commitment and render service to God. Our material possessions are the other means by which we show our love for God. So, if you have neither time nor money, what does that say about what you give God? The two parables in the twenty-fifth chapter of the Gospel of

Matthew, which form our text, address both sides of this coin — time and money. Either of these parables demands more attention than I will have time to give to it and more time than I know you want me to give to them.[1] Nevertheless, let me see if we cannot draw some highlights from each parable.

THE IMPORTANCE OF PREPARATION

Notice first the parable on time. The parable about the foolish and wise bridesmaids focuses on the efficient use of time and the necessity of preparing ahead of time for life's opportunities. One of the truths that leaps at me from this parable is the necessity of preparing for the good and happy occasions of life. Jesus said, "The Kingdom of God is like a wedding feast, so prepare to rejoice and be happy." Often we prepare for the hard times of life. We have often been exhorted: "Prepare for a rainy day." But we need also to prepare for good days. This we often do as we prepare for vacation time, anniversaries, birthdays, Christmas, special trips, college, or a wedding. We all need to make preparation for happy occasions as well as difficult times.

PREPARE FOR TESTING AND OPPORTUNITIES

This parable also focuses vividly on the importance of preparing for those times of testing and opportunities which come into a person's life. The French philosopher, Voltaire, has said, "I have noticed that destiny in every case depends upon the act of a moment." Many times what you and I become is a result of our response to an emergency or a crisis in our life. What are you really? It is revealed in that moment of testing or the opportunity that is thrust in your hand. Your response reveals what your real nature is like. A sailor may sail the sea year after year but his real sailing ability is revealed in a fierce storm. When one of our major airplanes had a part of its side blown away by a bomb, the pilot

---

1   For a careful study of these two parables see M. Eugene Boring, *Matthew: The New Interpreter's Bible* (Nashville: Abingdon Press, 1995), 451 ff.

demonstrated what kind of pilot he really was as he continued the flight and landed the plane safely in Hawaii. Times of testing come in our lives, and, as someone has observed, maybe, just maybe, the only real religion we have is what we call upon in a crisis! Failures, suffering, illness or grief come to us all. What do they reveal about our inner makeup?

When a man had given in to temptation, an older individual asked him: "Why, did you give in to it?" "You don't understand what external pressures were on me," the young man replied. "Where were your internal braces?" the older man asked. What we are like in an emergency is determined by what we have already put into our lives. A crisis exposes our inner nature. The fabric of our being is laid open in a moment.

PREPARE AHEAD OF TIME

The parable about the foolish young women also teaches that when the opportunities and times of testing come, it is too late to prepare then. In that moment we need action. Preparation has gone into our life years before you and I come to that moment. What we have put into our lives to form our ethical character is not arrived at and prepared for in that moment. What we have already built into our being determines who and what we are in that moment of decision. We foolishly think that we have always got time to prepare, but we do not. The years before that moment of testing prepare us for what is going to follow. What we are becoming is made clear in that time of testing. You cannot prepare for temptation, suffering, or adversity when you are facing the test. You prepare ahead of time. A sailor trims his ship in calm weather. We paint our house when the weather is beautiful and warm. We need to make preparation for times of difficulties when life is calm and good. When we do, we will be ready when the storms come.

CAN'T SHARE YOUR UNIQUE EXPERIENCE

Notice also that our text reveals that when one has prepared his or her life, one can't share that experience with someone else. The wise young women could not share their oil. This was not a matter of being stingy. Some things cannot be shared. Oh, you can talk to others about your experience. You may inspire them. But in your moment of testing, in your time of trial, I cannot give you my character. You must have your own. What you are within determines your response. A saint who has spent fifty years devoting his life in prayer to God cannot instantly give you his prayer life. A woman, who has spent ten years caring for an elderly husband, or a sick mother, cannot give to another her experience. When your time of trial, testing, or opportunity comes, no other individual can give you his or her character, strength, love, faith or hope. It is not transferable. You and I throughout our lives are determining who we are.

OPPORTUNITIES CAN'T BE RECALLED

The parable of the foolish young woman also teaches that opportunities usually cannot be recalled. Because the young women were unprepared, they found the door shut to them. There does come a time when the door is shut. When my children reached twenty-one, I could no longer relate to him or her as I could when he or she was three, or eight years old, or a teenager. Those opportunities are past. What I made of those moments was realized in those moments and cannot be experienced again at a later moment in exactly the same way. Into our lives many opportunities or trials come, and if we do not respond then, life moves on and we miss that moment to respond. Sometimes that opportunity can never be recaptured again. This opportunity or time of testing may be a chance to say a good word to a person, who needs encouragement, or to reach out a hand to somebody who is hurting, or visit a sick person, or comfort a grieving friend, or give your money to help support our church's ministry. Now is the right moment. Maybe this occasion will not come again. When the opportunity is missed, the door will be shut.

In the beautiful Lake District in England, there is a small village called Hawkshead where William Wordsworth attended school as a boy. In that village there is a small parish church named St. Michael. On the door of the church were written half printed and half scripted the following lines:

> *No man entering a house*
> *ignores him who dwells there*
> *This is the house of God*
> *and he is here*
> *Pray then to him who loves you*
> *and bids you welcome*
> *Give thanks*
> *for those who in years past*
> *built this place to his glory*
> *Rejoice*
> *in his gifts of beauty*
> *in art and music*
> *architecture and handicrafts*
> *and worship him*
> *the one God Father of us all*
> *through our Lord and Saviour*
> *Jesus Christ.*
> *Amen.*

OUR OPPORTUNITY IS NOW PRESENT

Our time is here. It is time to do our part in paying for our building expenses and ministries so that those who come after us can rejoice in its beauty and find it an oasis where they can worship and serve God. When our church's expenses are under written, our vision of ministry for God can be expanded in so many ways. We must not — cannot — miss our opportunity to do our part now.

THE SIGNIFICANCE OF TIME

Time. Time is like a flowing river that swiftly moves along carrying us from yesterday to tomorrow. Time is like a tunnel through which we walk from the past to the present. Time is like a mirror before which we see the passing parade of life. Time is a door which opens only toward the present or future. We cannot go backwards. Time is like stairs that carry us from the past to the future. Time is like an evasive rope that seems to be forever slipping out of our hands and is soon gone. Time is a challenge and an opportunity, joy and pain, hope and satisfaction, memory and action, pain and pleasure. How will we use it? This is your moment. Don't miss it!

The Proper Use of Our Possessions

The other parable in our text addresses the use of money. Talent was an unfortunate translation, because we think we can ignore it then, can't we? We quickly say: "Well, I don't have much talent for singing or teaching." But this parable was not talking about our talents but money. This parable was clearly about money, weights, or bags of gold. It focuses chiefly on the man who has any one bag of gold.

That encompasses so many of us, doesn't it? "Oh, I don't have much money," you say. "I am only one individual. What can I do?" "What difference will what I give make?" Yes, the man in Jesus' parable was given only one gift of money. But that one gift, some New Testament scholars project, might be worth in modern currency from seventy-five to a hundred and fifty thousand dollars. This may have been a working man's wages for twenty years. This was what he might earn working in his lifetime. The emphasis here was on a gift of money entrusted to a man which was equal to the money he might make in a lifetime. Let's follow this man's response to his challenge to use the money he is given.

OUR FEAR OF NOT HAVING ENOUGH MONEY

First, note that he was afraid. He was *afraid!* He seemed to be paralyzed by fear. But often so are you and I. We are afraid that we will never have enough money. If we give money to our church, we fear we may be misunderstood, criticized, or embarrassed. Our fear causes inertia. We can't respond because of our fears.

I read in the paper a number of years ago about a building that burned to the ground. This building was an icehouse. Inside the building was filled with frozen cubes of water, thousands of gallons of water to extinguish the flames. But they were not in an available form to put out the fire! The building was filled with frozen assets, but the building burned down because they were not available for use in their present mode. What a parable about the church! It is filled with frozen assets. Many remain frozen because they are afraid to use their gifts in God's work.

MISUNDERSTANDING GOD

Note also that the man in this parable misunderstood the nature of God. He thought that his owner was a harsh and cruel man. He feared him and said: "I must protect myself." Like this man, many go through life misunderstanding the nature of God and never give for the right reasons or never give at all because of their wrong attitude toward God. Others think that God just winks at what they do with their money. They do not realize that our use of our money and time reveal our attitude toward God. Our view of God determines our giving. Is it out of fear or love?

Did you hear about the man who wouldn't work? Someone asked him one day, "If your wife urged you to go out and look for a job, what would you look for?"

"I'd look for another wife!" he replied.

OUR RELATIONSHIP WITH GOD

Now that is a parable about some of us in our relationship with God. You know the Scripture is clear. Our time and our money reveal our attitude about God, but what do we do? We look for another God! We look for a God that will either reward us if we give or a God who doesn't care whether or not we give. So we fabricate another kind of God.

Observe that the man in this parable did nothing. He was not a criminal, nor was he a thief. He didn't waste his master's money. He just dug a hole in the ground and buried it. He did nothing. But, boy, a lot of folks today join his ranks, don't they? They do nothing. They have gifts. They have money. But they choose to do nothing with them for God. I am convinced that choosing to do nothing with your money is choosing. It makes a stand, and it stands against God. It stands in opposition to God's work. God challenges us to invest our time and money for Him. We select either to be for God or against Him. And in choosing not to do anything, we really choose to be against God.

A city dweller moved to the country and bought a cow. He didn't know anything about milking a cow. So in a few weeks his cow went dry. He commented to one of his neighboring farmers: "You know, I just do not understand it. I didn't abuse this cow at all. When I didn't need any milk, I didn't milk her. If I only needed a quart, that is all I took. I just don't understand it. After a while she just dried up." The farmer told him that you get milk from a cow by getting all the milk that you can every day from the cow. By doing nothing and not milking the cow completely every day caused the cow to go dry. Some of us do not understand that our lives become dry spiritually because we try to give God just a little or nothing of our money. Then we wonder why we slowly dry up spiritually.

EXCUSES FOR NOT USING THE MONEY CORRECTLY

The man in our parable offered all kinds of excuses, didn't he? "My master is hard and harsh," he said. But we have excuses, too. The list is endless. We have so many bills to pay, things to do, how can we possibly give money to church and God? We do so by determining priorities, don't we? That is important.

FAITHFULNESS ENLARGES OPPORTUNITY

Notice what happened in this parable to the men who were faithful. They enlarged their companionship. The men who used their money wisely had fellowship with each other. Notice also there was increased opportunity. Those who invested their money wisely didn't find themselves free of responsibility. They were given more opportunities to serve and expand their gifts.

RECEIVING THE DELIGHT OF GOD

They also received the joy of God. What is that joy? Is it that God will make you rich and famous? No! I don't believe that we give for that reason. The joy of the Lord is enough to hear Him say, "Well done." Imagine standing before the throne of God and receiving from Him the words: "Well done, my good and faithful servant."

What more could we ask for? When you stand before the throne of God, what will you tell Christ about your use of time and money? Will you say to Christ: "Oh, God, you know I meant to get around to giving my time and money to You at some point? But, You know, I never really had enough time or money to do anything I really wanted to do. So I just decided to wait and wait and wait."

Every single one of us has a place. We have time and money. Generations from now some persons may ask you, "What did you do at the time your church had a special need to pay for its building and support its ministries?" Can you say that you kept your face against the challenge and you dug deeply into your personal recourses and did your part? God grant that we shall all be faithful.

Eternal God, who has loved us with an everlasting love, teach us how to be faithful in our use of time and money. Through Christ, who sacrificed all for us, we pray. Amen.

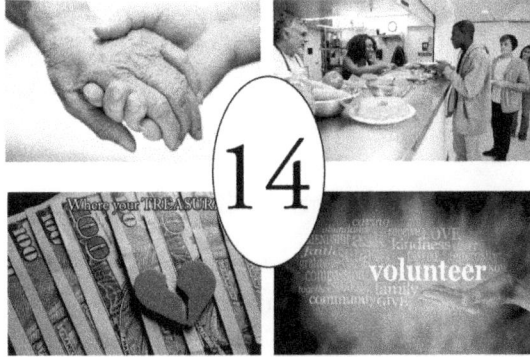

"WHEN MONEY HAS US TALKING TO OURSELVES"

Luke 12:13-21

We use the phrase, "Money talks" often. What we mean by that is we are able to get results with money. You may have heard about the man who was admitted into the Metropolitan Hospital in New York City. He had swallowed over three hundred coins — quarters, nickels, dimes, and pennies. But nobody knew why. Obviously he had to be hospitalized. A minister who heard about this episode said: "Well, here is a man who finally put his money where his mouth was!" There are indeed a lot of folks who consume money in many ways.

FOCUSING ON ONE'S SELF

In the parable taken from the Gospel of Luke, Jesus speaks about the man whose money had him talking to himself. We listen in on his soliloquy. Notice as he begins his conversation how he focuses upon himself. "I said to myself." His money has him talking to himself. "I said to myself," the certain rich man thought. "What will I do? I already have great possessions and many barns, but they will not house all that I possess. What can I do?" In this parable the rich man emphasizes "I" or "me" six times. Six other times he uses "my" or "your" in talking about his own possessions. The emphasis is on "I" and "me." Kenneth Bailey reminds us that this man was not a very good Jew. No Jewish man made decisions isolated and alone. He went to the city gate and dialogued with his fellow Jews. He made decisions in conversations with others and not by himself.[1] This process of isolation indicates his selfishness.

MEASURING LIFE BY OUR POSSESSIONS

The rich man thought his possessions could give him real meaning in life. He measured his life by what he had instead of by who he was. Many of us unfortunately measure our lives like that. We think that the things we own give us our meaning in life. What a tragic perception of what makes us a meaningful person. This man would be judged successful by the world's standards. There is no mention that he earned his money dishonestly. He is certainly prudent to be making preparation for the future. He is thoughtful to protect his investment. That is not the issue. His problem was his focus on "things."

Many of you have seen the play or movie *Fiddler on the Roof*. Do you remember when Tevye sings a song about his daydream to be rich? Tevye, the milkman, who is the leading character in the play, sings: "If I were a rich man, daidle, diedle, daidle ... All day long I'd biddy, biddy bum. If I were a wealthy man! I wouldn't have to work hard, daidle, deedle ... If I were a biddy, biddy rich I'd build a big tall house with rooms by the dozen right in the middle of town. A fine tin roof with real wooden floors below. There could be one long staircase just going up and one even longer coming down. One more leading nowhere just for show. I'd fill my yards with chicks and turkeys and geese and ducks for the town to see and hear. Squawking just as noisily as they can. And each loud quack and cluck and gobble and honk would land like a trumpet on the ear — as if to say, here lives a wealthy man."[2]

---

1   Kenneth E. Bailey, *Through Peasant Eyes* (Grand Rapids, Michigan: Wm. E. Eerdmans, 1980), 65.

2   Sheldon Harnick and Jerry Bock, "If I Were A Rich Man" (from Fiddler on the Roof) in *Songwriters Now and Then* (Charles Hansen Educational Music and Books, Inc., 1973), 60-62.

If I were a rich man, I would have meaning, happiness, and joy. Here in this parable are the reflections of a certain rich man. Before you quickly dismiss yourself from the lesson of this parable, because you think it points to somebody else — a rich man, remember … every single one of us here in this church is a rich person. By the world's standards, we are all wealthy. The rich man's sin was revealed as he talked to himself. His focus was on himself.

CAN POSSESSIONS GIVE US HAPPINESS?

Notice, secondly, that the rich man is saying to himself that his possessions will bring him happiness. "I will say to my soul, 'Enjoy yourself, take it easy, let your possessions give you meaning. Riches will let you take it easy.'" Many people long to be rich persons so they can take it easy and not have to struggle or work in life. But God has so constructed our universe that struggle and labor are a part of it. When a person has no job, no work that gives satisfaction, and does not do anything to give life meaning, then that individual is usually not happy. Happiness often is found through struggle.

A man happened to see a butterfly as it was slowly beginning to break out of its chrysalis. He could see the wings trying to push their way through the cocoon. He watched the butterfly in its struggle to free itself and felt sorry for the creature. It was trying so hard to get out, but it seemed to be making little progress. Finally, he decided he would help the butterfly. So he took his pocketknife and slowly cut some slits in the chrysalis so the butterfly could slip through. And it did. Soon, however, he noticed that the butterfly did not seem to be as strong as it should be. The colors on the wings were not as beautiful. Within a few hours he noticed that the butterfly was dead. A part of the essential developing process for the butterfly came in its struggle to get free of the cocoon.

Life loses meaning when all struggle is gone. No one simply finds life meaningful, but one makes life worthwhile. That often involves struggle against evil and pain. Struggle is usually involved in our working, growing, maturing, and developing in life. Without struggle we cannot reach the potential for which we have been created.

This rich man thought that his possessions could give him happiness. He mistakenly assumed that he could be content with what gave his body satisfaction. He thought to himself that physical things could enrich his life and fill it with meaning. This philosophy is seen on television, in magazines and movies all the time. We are bombarded with the view that things, things, THINGS fulfill us and give us life's real meaning. But it is a lie and do not buy into it.

He also echoed the lie that he had all the time he wanted. He thought he had plenty of time to build his barns and then enjoy life at his own leisure. He took tomorrow for granted. Many of us live our lives with the assumption that we have all of the time in the world to do whatever it is that we desire. However, we have no promise like that at all from God.

JESUS DEPICTS THE RICH MAN'S ATTITUDE AS FOOLISH

In the third place, we observe that God enters into the dialogue and addresses the rich man as a fool. The rich man thought his life could be centered around things — what he had — what he possessed. The Bible speaks about prayer over five hundred times. It also speaks of faith over five hundred times. But it speaks about a person's possessions and their relationship to his religion over a thousand times. Sixteen of Jesus' parables focus on what a person does with his or her possessions. The Bible challenges us to take seriously the significance of our possessions and their impact on our spiritual development.

There is a children's story which has a deep meaning for all of us. There was a nightingale that had become a bit lazy. A peddler made a deal with the nightingale to give her a worm for one feather so she wouldn't have to work. Ah, that seemed such a marvelous bargain, didn't it? Just one feather for a worm. Each day the nightingale gave up another feather for a worm. Finally, she got to the point she could not fly. Then one morning the nightingale met the peddler. She had worked all night long digging enough worms to pay the peddler back. "I have enough worms now to buy back my feathers," she said. "My dear," the peddler said, "my business is worms for feathers, not feathers for worms!"

You can't buy back what you have given up. When you sell your soul to things, you cannot buy it back. Jesus said that life does not consist in the abundance of things. This means that you cannot give your first priority to things. This doesn't mean that you have to give up everything, but you are challenged to find the more abundant life. You cannot spend your whole life focusing on accumulating "things" and come to the end of your life on earth and expecting to enter the next life with spiritual values being number one. Make a decision now that you will make spiritual matters first in your life and that your possessions will be used in such a way as to enable you to reach that goal.

LIFE'S MEANING FOCUSES ON INWARD CHARACTER

What does life consist of? Life doesn't consist of just what we have — not cash but character — not possessions but personhood. Life consists in what a person *knows*. This focuses on what you have accumulated within. It emphasizes your awareness of things as they have an impact on **persons**. We are part of all we have met, where we have been, what we have read, studied and learned. Our life has been dyed by the whole process of living which has brought us to this moment. We are who we know and what we know.

In *Alice in Wonderland*, Alice meets the Cheshire Cat and asks him: "Would you tell me, please which way I ought to go from here?"

"That depends a good deal on where you want to get to," he responds.

"I don't much care where" Alice replies.

"Then it doesn't matter which way you go," said the cat.

If you don't have any direction for your life, you cannot control the way you will go. You just flow with the stream. Jesus said,

"I have come that you might have life and have it abundantly." To know Jesus Christ is to have eternal life. To know Jesus is to have direction and purpose. Life consists in what we know.

MEANING REFLECTED IN WHAT ONE DOES

Life also consists in what a person *does.* What are you doing with your life? What gives fulfillment to you? What have you committed your life to? Have you committed your life simply to building greater barns? To have more and more? Or have you committed your life to building your own inner person? You have found meaning not merely in what you have – what you possess, but in who you are. This means that you have to set priorities in your life. You have to determine what will be first in your life. You need to have God first in your life. One of the ways you do that is by setting the priority of your family budget to put God first. You can tell how important the church, Christ, and God are to a person by looking at his or her checkbooks. What we write our checks for reveal how seriously we take God and our religion. I hope that you will build some spiritual meaning in your life and not give it just to material things.

Sigmund Freud loved to tell the story about a shipwrecked sailor who was found by some islanders and carried back to their village on their shoulders. The sailor thought they were going to have him for lunch, but instead they put a crown on his head and made him king. They gave him everything he ever asked for and met his every need. He had never had such a marvelous time. After a few months, however, he began to be a bit worried about this kingly life. He asked somebody what it meant. They told him that their custom was to pick one person to crown as king for a year. For that whole year the person got everything he wanted. But at the end of that year they banished him to an island where he would starve to death. The sailor began to think about what he might do. What he did was to instruct the islanders to take boats over to the island of banishment and plant fruit trees. He ordered them to build a house there for him. He got them to plow a garden and plant crops. He ordered them to put other provisions he might need for the future. When his year came to an end and they sent him to this island, he had prepared for his future.

Jesus warns us in this parable, "Prepare for the future. One day you will stand before the eternal God of the universe. Whose will these possessions be then, since you have focused your life on them and have done nothing to prepare for the life to come?" Life consists of what one does. What are you doing with what you have to prepare for the life beyond this one?

MEANING REFLECTED IN WHAT ONE LOVES

Life also consists in what one *loves*. What is your first love? To what have you committed your life? Possessions and things? Or have you given yourself to Christ and His Church and ministering in His name? What is your love? Your first love reveals your real priorities in living.

A number of years ago, when they were constructing the Washington Monument, a man visited one of his neighbors in Virginia and tried to solicit some money from the farmer for the monument. The man said to him, "I can't see any point in building a monument to Washington out there. I'll keep Washington in my heart and remember him there."

"You are going to keep him in a very tight place," the friend replied.

There are a lot of people in church who do the same thing. They talk about how much they love their church, how much it means to them, but they give almost nothing. They live on the church but do not give to the church to be a part of those who support the work of Christ. I am giving my tithe to the budget of this church and will be giving to the *Together We Share Program* in a sacrificial way above my tithe. I am giving so the debt of this church can be removed, and we can get on with its ministry. My dream is that one day we will be giving to missions an amount equal to what we have paid for the debt of this church. But we will never be able to give to missions as we want to until we finish this debt. Let's get that obligation behind us.

As you are preparing to give, remember the ministries of this church — the ministries of counseling, in nursing homes, to the unemployed, to the hurting and needy, to the hospitalized, to those on mission fields, to the young, to the children, to the old, to families, singles, and countless others. Think of the numerous ministries which this church has because you are willing to give. Don't deny yourself that opportunity. Show your love by being a part of those who give. Remember the words of Jesus about a certain rich man — that is you — you and me — we are all rich persons here today. Jesus gives us a warning in this parable not to commit our lives to things but to God.

A small five-year-old boy went to his first day in kindergarten. He walked around and looked at the small chairs and small tables. He studied the coat rack which was at his height. Even the bathroom was designed to meet his size. He walked over to his teacher and said in a disgusted way: "I don't like this place."

She asked, "Why?"

"There is nothing here to grow to," he replied.

In God's Kingdom we are all children. God is pulling us upward to grow beyond material ends. God is challenging us to let spiritual values be the chief center of our lives. We are summoned to put first the Kingdom of God. We are to grow to be like God. God grant that each of us will have eyes to see and ears to hear.

All Loving God, we thank You for Your love. May we love You by showing it in what we do and say, and in how we give. Through Christ we pray. Amen.

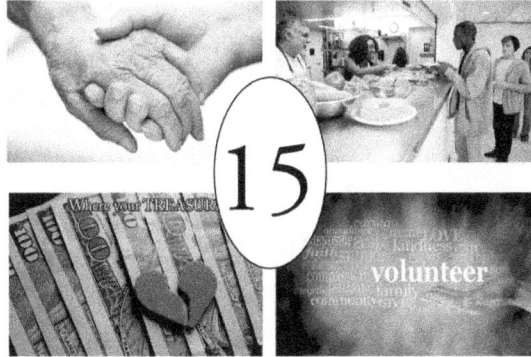

"EXTRAVAGANT LOVE"

Mark 14:1-9

Several years ago on Halloween, a church group was out doing their annual Trick or Treat for UNICEF. The young people walked up to the door of a luxurious house and rang the doorbell. A man came to the door. When the young people told him their reason for being there, he exclaimed: "I never give to anything! Go away!"

Contrast that experience with the story in our biblical text. Mark interrupted his story about the Passover and Jesus' journey to His crucifixion to give an account of a woman who anointed Jesus. The scene takes place in the little town of Bethany at the home of Simon, designated as a leper, obviously a former leper. Three other gospels report this same story. John's Gospel identifies the woman with the alabaster box as Mary, the sister of Martha, who prepared a meal while Mary sat listening at Jesus' feet, and Lazarus, whom Jesus raised from the grave.

Picture the scene in your mind. Jesus and the others present for the meal were reclining around the low table on benches, or possibly even on the floor. Mary enters the room bearing a very expensive flask of alabaster which may have been her own burial ointment. Mark indicates that was a costly gift, worth about three hundred denarii. That was equivalent to a working man's wages for a whole year. That was a very expensive bottle of perfume! She breaks the bottle and anoints the head of Jesus. Luke states that she poured the ointment on Jesus' feet. It is possible she anointed both His head and feet. The aroma filled the room. Down through the centuries the fragrance of that act has continued to touch the lives of persons. Let's look at this story, thousands of years old, and see if it has a message for us today.

THE MOTIVE FOR GIVING

First, notice the motive of the woman who broke the alabaster bottle and anointed the head and feet of Jesus. "She has done a beautiful thing for me," Jesus said. Her motive for this act was one of love and gratitude for Jesus. If this is Mary, the sister of Lazarus, as the Gospel of John states, then this act was an extravagant expression of her gratitude to Jesus for bringing her brother back from the dead. Lazarus, who had recently been dead, was sitting with the other guests.

HER MOTIVE MISUNDERSTOOD

Notice that immediately her motive is misunderstood. Whispers begin to be heard among the people. The whispers of discontent quickly poisoned the minds of the guests. They condemned her with indignant looks and critical words. "How could she waste so much money?" John said that it was Judas who led the criticism but the other gospel writers indicate that the disciples and the other guests as well engaged in the conversation about the waste of this act.

"Why such a waste?" they asked. Their behavior revealed something about their own material standards and values as well as their inability to perceive what Jesus saw in this woman's action. Judas and the others saw nothing to praise, only to condemn. They saw this as a foolish waste of money. Imagine a year's wages invested in something that produces an odor for a moment. They had nothing but a sweet smell when there were poor people just down the street who needed food. To them such a waste was not only foolish but wicked. Jesus observed that the kindness to the poor was always possible. This opportunity would not always be there.

EXTRAVAGANT LOVE

Mary's action was one of extravagant love. Jesus was at a critical moment in His life. He knew that He was going toward Jerusalem and that His death was imminent. It was important for Him to know if there was anyone in the group of His disciples or other followers who had really heard Him and understood what His ministry was all about. Was there anyone? Then this woman stepped forward and anointed His head and feet, and Jesus realized that someone had understood His message. He had come to win the love of people, and here in this act where Mary poured her ointment upon Jesus to express her love and gratitude, He realized that He had won a place in the heart of at least one person.

The First Epistle of John observes, "We love because he has first loved us" (1 John 4:15). "God commended his love toward us while we were yet sinners, Christ died for us" (Romans 5:8). Jesus said, "Come unto me all you who are weak and heavy laden" (Matthew 11:28). "I, if I be lifted up," Jesus exclaimed, "I will draw all persons unto me" (John 12:32). Paul declared, "For me to live is Christ" (Philippians 1:21). The Christian faith is not founded merely on ideas, theologies, philosophies, systems, or institutions. It rests on a commitment to the person of Jesus Christ. "The love of Christ," Paul declares, "constrains us" (2 Corinthians 5:1). Our faith rests on a commitment to Christ, and Mary indicated that she had made that kind of commitment.

A woman was visiting a friend one day and she was accompanied by her two children. After the two women had talked awhile and the friend had gotten to observe the two children's behavior, she commented: "I would give my life to have two children like that."

The mother observed with a smile, "And that is exactly what it costs!"

The act of devotion by Mary cost the commitment of her life. The greatest gifts are sacrificial gifts. The Christian life begins with a costly commitment of one's self to Jesus Christ.

Praise from Jesus

Her action won praise from our Lord. The New Testament contains a short list of the times Jesus praised the action of people. He praised the widow who dropped in her tiny mite in the offering box at the temple, and observed that she had given her all. He praised a centurion for his faith. "I have not seen such faith in all of Israel," Jesus noted. And now this woman received His words of praise. She had exercised spontaneous love. Her expression of love could not be censured or confined. Her action broke normal patterns and seemed to defy common sense. Nevertheless, it was her profound expression of extravagant love.

Tennyson expresses Mary's devotion in these pictorial words:

"Her eyes are homes of silent prayer,
Nor other thought her mind admits
But, 'He was dead, and there he sits,
And he that brought him back is there.'

"Then one deep love doth supersede
All other, when her ardent gaze
Roves from the living brother's face
And rests upon the Life indeed.

"All subtle thought, all curious fears,
Borne down by gladness so complete,.
She bows, she bathes the Saviour's feet
With costly spikenard and with tears."

(In Memoriam xxx11)

A Beautiful Thing

"Leave her alone," Jesus declared. "She has done a beautiful thing for me." It is so hard for some of us who are pragmatic and practical persons to understand how what seemed like a waste could be praiseworthy. These persons have difficulty in seeing the beauty and graciousness of love. But down through the centuries, this kind of act has been duplicated by Christians. Thousands of small country churches and giant cathedrals have been built as places of worship out of love for Jesus Christ. This kind of love has inspired the gifts of memorial stained glass windows, pipe organs, communion sets, choir robes, musical chimes and countless other items. Sometimes at special seasons of the year like Christmas, the pulpit area in churches has been decorated with hundreds of poinsettias, and at Easter lilies have blanketed the front of churches. Out of love for Christ, great music has been composed; moving poems, breathtaking art and profound theological books have been produced.

Why Give Money to Church Buildings?

Why such "waste?" How can Christians build buildings like our church structures? Why not give all of the money this building cost to the poor? Why have Christians chosen to make such gifts? The question of Judas is still with us. I can remember raising it myself! A pragmatic view of life may blind us to see that the expression of an overflowing heart may be lavish at times. This question is answered when we realize that the church is the base for doing ministry. Through the ages the Christian Church has been the base for reaching out to the poor, and those who needed other kinds of help. How many hospitals do you know that have been founded by agnostics and atheists? How many children's homes, homes for the elderly, alcohol and drug centers, or other institutions have been established by agnostics and atheists to help others? This kind of generous concern has continued to arise out of the desire of the church to help those in need. The church is the fountain which sends a rushing stream of love that flows throughout the world to reach others for Christ and to show His love and concern..

I have often wished that every single member of our church would receive and read the brochure we give to our Sunday visitors. I am astounded that so many people in our congregation are totally unaware of the vast number and variety of ministries within this church. Let me share with you in a small nutshell something of the "fragrance" which flows from the many ministries in our church. The programs and ministries I am about to list are in addition to the "nuts and bolts" operations like Sunday School, WMU causes and our regular organizations. Listen to this list:

In music, we have several preschool choirs, one of which you heard this morning, a middle and senior high school choir, our sanctuary choir, children, youth, and adult handbell choirs and an orchestra. In addition to our regular Sunday School classes for young people, there is Top Priority, weekend retreats, basketball, softball, and other sporting activities. We have many community and world-wide mission activities. Some of these are conducted through our WMU or Sunday School classes. In addition to these we have a Sunday worship radio ministry, a ministry to fifteen nursing homes, the Wayne Oates Pastoral Counseling Center, a clothes closet, a food pantry, a Job Club Center that reaches throughout our community and city to help train and equip people and locate jobs for them. We sponsor an Alzheimer's Share Care Program. There is a plaque out in the vestibule on the table which we received yesterday from the Alzheimer group in recognition and appreciation for this church's ministry and support of those who are concerned about those who suffer with Alzheimer's disease in our community.

The list continues: A Hispanic Mission, Operation HUGG — that reaches out to our homebound members — Second Family Program, an adoption program for newcomers to the area, support groups for widows and widowers, personal growth groups, and support groups for divorced persons. We also sponsor support groups for blended families, marriage preparation classes, marriage retreats, parenting skills seminars. And Friends for Life, a new cancer support group, has just been founded. Our children's ministries include Sunday School classes and Children's Worship, RA's, GA's, discipleship classes, Morning Madness — a summer activity for children — Bible Drill and Vacation Bible School. For preschoolers, we have weekday kindergarten, nursery school, St. MAM Day Care, Mother's Day Out, and Mission Friends. For single adults in our church there are groups like the New Horizons, for those who are divorced; New Friends, for those who are recently widowed; monthly singles sinners, single adult seminars, and there is the Grandview Club for senior citizens. In addition to these, we have ceramic classes, gymnastics, exercise programs, t-ball, dart ball, and many others. We also sponsor many special seminars and conferences. Our cooperative fund giving and other mission gifts support the work of the Long Run Baptist Association, Kentucky Baptists, Kentuckiana Interfaith Community, St. MAM, the Cooperative Baptist Fellowship, the Baptist World Alliance, and others.

If you are not proud of the wide and varied work and ministry of this church, you simply don't understand it. And these are just a part of our total work. I know of no church anywhere, ANYWHERE, that does the variety and scope of the ministries of St. Matthews Baptist Church. One of the pledges which many of us made when we came into this great building was that it would be used as much as possible for ministry. Any day you come to this building you will see it filled with life. Persons, activities, programs of all kinds and ministries of all descriptions will be going on. We can take great pride in the work and ministries of St. Matthews Baptist Church.

GIVE OUT OF DEVOTION TO CHRIST

Mary's stewardship sprang from a devoted love of Christ. You and I ought to give to Christ and His church out of love and gratitude. That's the main reason to give. We give our tithe to church because that is our way of saying that we love God and want to do our part to help this church carry on the ministries of Christ. "Leave her alone," Jesus said of Mary, "she has given her best." Her gift was born out of love. Her thought was what she could do for Jesus and not herself. Nothing which is born from the motive of selfishness is beautiful. We tithe not for what we can get out of it but from a desire to give. We give not for reward but to express love. Giving to Christ through His church is the Christian's way of saying that he or she is not a slave to material things. It is our way of demonstrating Christ's control of our lives.

A small boy wrote a note to God and stuck it in an offering envelope and placed it in the collection plate when it was passed in church. The note was given to the pastor. The note read: "Dear God, I love You. Do You love me? Answer yes." Our programs and ministries in this church are varied ways our church tries to say to the world, "We love you. And in the name of Jesus Christ, we want to minister to you."

THE MEASURE OF MARY'S GIVING

Secondly, look at the measure of Mary's giving. The measurement of her love was seen in her sacrificial love. Jesus said, "She has done what she could." Or this phrase might be translated, "What she had she did." Jesus didn't say that Mary gave everything that she had. She gave the best gift she had at that time. She honestly did what she could to try to please God. She took advantage of the opportunity of that moment to give the very best that she had in that situation. She didn't try to preach. She didn't try to teach. She didn't even cook the meal. Her sister was probably the one who did that. But she shared what she had. She gave her own gift. She was herself. This gift was her way of showing love and devotion to Christ.

She took advantage of the opportunity which lay before her. This was her moment to act. A moment like this might not come along again, and so spontaneously she expresses her love. There are many of us who sit around and say: "Well, when the right moment comes, I'll do something for Christ and His church." The right moment is the opportunity at hand. Whenever and wherever the moment or occasion comes to serve Christ, seize that moment. It may not arise just like that again. Nicodemus and Joseph of Arimathea provided Jesus with a place to be buried, but they missed an opportunity to take a stand with Him before He was crucified. That moment would never come again. Many deeds are missed because persons do not take advantage of the opportunities they have at hand. Mary's generous impulse was used and not lost. If some opportunities are put off until tomorrow, they will be lost forever.

Mary didn't calculate how she would give her gift. The ointment she poured on Jesus' body was likely what she was saving for her own burial. She shared all that she had in that particular gift. She didn't say, "Well, I'll take this one bottle of alabaster and I'll put a few drops on Jesus." The only way that particular bottle could be used was to break open the neck of the bottle. Once it was broken open, all of the contents were poured out. She didn't say, "I'll see what little bit I can get by with or what is the least I can use?" Her love was unmeasured. She didn't hold back. She did the best that she could with what she had to honor Christ. Life passes some people by as they calculate what few drops will be required. Rather than holding back, Mary gave all she had in that moment.

Some people daydream, "If I had a million dollars, I could remove our church's debt." Well, you wouldn't remove our debt, but that would certainly help. Too many play the game of "if only…" That's like sitting around and saying, "If wishes were fishes, we could all fill our dishes." But we are not going to solve our church debt or financial problems that way. Our financial load will be resolved by each member of our congregation committing his or her gifts to God. We began with a building indebtedness of four million dollars. Our debt is now 3.4 million. Through your faithfulness in giving, we have already reduced the principal by six hundred thousand dollars. No millionaires did this for us. You and I did it through our sacrificial gifts. As we continue to give faithfully, our debt will be decreased.

Our operating budget is supported by the faithfulness of our members. The deacons, Sunday School teachers, Budget Planning Committee, and the staff — eighty-seven persons-have already pledged a third of the amount needed for our church budget. Eighty-seven family units have underwritten thirty-two percent of the budget. This church has about a thousand family units. Can you think what our budget ought to be if our church members tithed and gave faithfully? Our budget is only a fraction of what it should be if all our members did his or her part as this woman did in sharing what she had with Jesus.

There is a beautiful children's book, which speaks to adults as well entitled *The Giving Tree* by Shel Silverstein. It is the story about a tree and a boy. Every day the little boy would play in the tree. He would climb the tree, play in its branches, and gather its leaves, eat its apples and sit in the shade of the tree. The boy loved the tree, and the tree was happy.

As time went by, the little boy grew older and the tree was often alone. Then one day the boy came back. The tree said, "Come, boy, and play with me."

"I'm too big to climb and play," said the boy. "I want to buy things and have fun. I want some money."

"I'm sorry," the tree said, "but I have no money. Take my apples and sell them and get some money." The boy did and the tree was happy.

A few years later the boy came back to the tree and told him that he needed to build a house. The tree said, "I have no house, but you may cut off my branches and build a house." The boy did, and the tree was happy.

The boy stayed away a long time and came back years later as an older man. He is depressed, sad and old. "I want a boat that will take me far away from here."

"Cut down my trunk and make a boat, then you can sail away." He did and the tree was happy.

Years later, the boy now an old man who is bent over with age comes back to the tree. "I'm sorry, boy," said the tree, "but I have nothing left to give you. My apples are gone. My branches are gone. My trunk is gone... I have nothing left. I am just an old stump. I am sorry."

The old man said, "I don't need much now, just a quiet place to sit and rest."

"Well," said the tree, "an old stump is good for sitting and resting. Come, boy, sit down. Sit down and rest." And the boy did, and the tree was happy.[1]

Sometimes there are individuals who give everything they have. We have persons in this congregation who have done that. We have some staff persons in this church who have worked for years with no raises or only modest raises so our church could continue in its ministry. Our Children's Minister has worked twelve years and the Minister of Pastoral Care has served for seven and a half years. The Pastor's Secretary has worked for twelve years and the Financial Secretary has worked for twenty-one years. All of the staff has served our church sacrificially. There are laypersons in this church who have given sacrificially of their time and money. They at times must feel like "the giving tree." There are others in our congregation who have received much but have been unwilling to give. Each of us needs to hear God's call to share in the giving load of his church. Each bears a part of the total load.

On his Election Day broadcast, which included a new President of the United States, Paul Harvey observed: "Demographics are such that the number of Americans listening to my voice right now could determine the outcome of today's election.... simply by choosing, one by one, not to vote." As with the election of our President, so it is with the stewardship responsibility of our church, by choosing to do nothing you can determine the outcome of the ministry of our church. Your pledge, your support -one by one — makes all of the difference in our church's ministry. Are you bearing your part of the load? Mary gave what she had. You have an opportunity. The challenge is yours.

---

1 Shel Silverstein, *The Giving Tree* (New York: Harper & Row, 1964).

MARY'S ANOINTING WAS A PROPHETIC STATEMENT

Finally notice the meaning of this story. Jesus said, "She has anointed my body beforehand for its burial." I am not certain that Mary understood all that she was doing when she broke that bottle and anointed Jesus' head. Did she realize what she was doing? I think she realized who Jesus was before the disciples — the men — came to that insight. I think that this woman, who sat at Jesus' feet, perceived through His teachings that this was the *Messiah*, the anointed one, which is what the word *Messiah* means. This was her way of anointing Him as the *Messiah*. Her action was a prophetic word, an anticipatory act about the one who would suffer and die for our redemption.

Whenever the church gathers at the Communion Table it celebrates the costly gift of God's sacrifice for us through the death of His son, Jesus Christ. We will remember that costly sacrifice every time we commune at His table.

D. T. Niles tells the story about a man named Mathew Sands, a retired pastor, who received a telegram in World War II that his son was missing in action and was likely dead. After reflecting for awhile on the message of the telegram, he turned it over and wrote across the back: "All that I have and all that I am, I give to God and for His service." These words of recommitment brought some comfort to his grieving spirit. A short time later he received a telephone call inviting him to do some teaching at a nearby university. As he was driving to the university, he stopped at an abandoned church. A sign in the church yard read: "For sale by auction." He went inside and looked at the church and prayed. He decided that day that he was going to buy the church and restore it to its mission.

While he was there another man, who wanted to buy the church and turn it into "Andy's Amusement Arcade," came by to appraise the property. Sands decided to send the trustees a bid for the church property. On Saturday he gathered with a curious group of people for the auction. While he was standing there waiting for the auction to begin, he reached in his pocket and pulled out the bid he thought he had sent to the trustees. He realized that he had accidentally sent the telegram from the war department instead. He was disgusted with himself and got ready to leave. But he decided to stay anyway. The trustees from the church stood up and said that they had decided to sell to the highest bidder. The highest bidder they announced was Mathew Sands. They read aloud his bid. "All that I have and all I am, I give to God for His service."

What more can we give God than that? Are you willing to make that kind of sacrifice?

Lord, may we be willing to give sacrificially to advance Your ministry through our church. Give us the courage to give extravagantly. Amen.

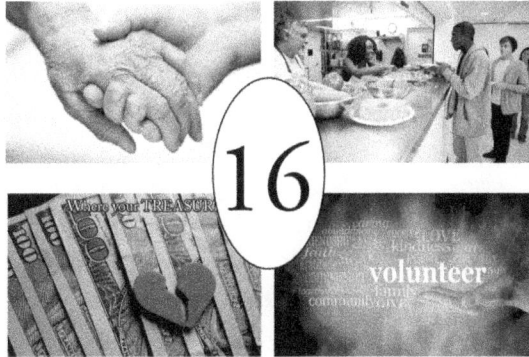

"CHECKING YOUR INVESTMENTS AND RETURNS"

Luke 12:13-23; 2 Corinthians 9:1-15

On a small farm near Hastings, Nebraska, an interesting episode occurred late one night that communicates a motivating moral to me. A chicken farmer had made a small opening in the bottom of his fence for a bantam rooster to go and come as he desired. On this particular night a half-grown coyote wandered by the farm and discovered that small opening in the fence. By using all the efforts he could, he squeezed through the tiny hole into the chicken lot. He had a feast and gorged himself on six hens that night. After eating all he could hold, he tried to squeeze back through the hole. But he couldn't! He was too big. He was trapped! The next morning the farmer found him in his chicken yard and shot him. His greediness had killed him.

When I first read that story, it immediately became a parable to me about human covetousness. Many of us become imprisoned by things. Soon our possessions possess us. The lure of money destroys marriages, families, businesses, and sometimes whole communities. Our quest for money sometimes causes ulcers, heart attacks, unbelievable stress, and creates workaholism. The lure of money often leads to an early death.

THE DANGER OF COVETOUSNESS

Jesus warns His followers on numerous occasions about the dangers of covetousness. The man in the crowd mentioned in Luke 12:13-14, who provoked the parable about the rich man from our Lord's lips, approached Jesus because he wanted Him to give a new interpretation of the law. This man was following a common custom in that day to ask a rabbi to interpret the law for him. But Jesus knew that this man understood what the law was.

The law was clear on this matter. At the death of the father the oldest son received two-thirds of the estate. If there was another son or sons, he or they received an equal part of the remaining one-third. This son, however, was not satisfied with his share. He wanted more. He was covetous and wanted Jesus to help him satisfy his drive. The parable of the rich fool was given as a warning against covetousness.

In the Scriptures there are more than five hundred references to prayer. There are almost five hundred references to faith. But there are over a thousand references in the Scriptures to a person's relationship to his possessions and how that relationship can affect his faith in God. Sixteen of Jesus' parables are concerned with how an individual uses his or her possessions. Jesus warns us in ringing words: "Beware of covetousness." "Lay not up for yourselves treasures on earth." "You cannot serve God and mammon." "It is easier," he said, "for a camel to go through the eye of a needle than for a rich man to enter the Kingdom of God." "A man's life does not consist in the abundance of the things he possesses." "What does it profit a man, if he gains the whole world, and loses his soul?"

MEASURING BY OUR POSSESSIONS

We often measure a person by his or her possessions. We sometimes hear the question raised: "How much do you think he is worth?" Now, what do we mean by that? Oh, you know what a person means by that. They are asking: "How much money does he have?" "How many possessions does he or she have?" We often measure a person's worth by the number of cars, houses, the size of his or her bank account, certificates of deposits, and stocks and bonds they have. The financial worth of an individual becomes the way of measuring his or her worth. Our possessions are supposed to determine who and what we are.

GUARDING AGAINST GREED

Jesus warns us to guard against all kinds of greed. Greed is a selfish standard of measurement. The rich man in the parable Jesus told had invested everything he had selfishly. He measured his life by what he had. Notice the dialogue the rich man had with himself in the parable in Luke 12:16-21. Six times in this parable he refers to "my" barns, "my" crops, and "my" soul. Six times "I" echoes through this parable. His life is centered inward. The words, "said to himself," literally might be translated from the Greek to read: "He dialogues with himself." He carried on a conversation with himself. That approach would have gone against the normal Jewish tradition. A Jewish man would go to the city gate and engage in dialogue with others before he made an important decision. His dialogue with himself had separated him from others. He had lost sight that possessions are means toward a greater end and were not an end in themselves. His greed made him short-sighted.

Have you heard about the advertisement that appeared in an American newspaper in 1875? The ad read like this:

> GLORIOUS OPPORTUNITY TO GET RICH. We are starting a cat ranch in Lacon (ILL.) with 100,000 cats. Each cat will average 12 kittens a year. The cat skins will sell for 30 cents each. One hundred men can skin 5,000 cats a day. We figure a daily profit of over $10,000. Now what shall we feed the cats? We will start a rat ranch next door with one million rats. The rats will breed 12 times faster than the cats. So we will have four rats to feed each day to each cat. Now what shall we feed the rats? We will feed the rats the carcasses of the cats after they have been skinned. Now Get This! We feed the rats to the cats and the cats to the rats and get the skins for nothing.

How many of us want that kind of approach in life? That is the reason the lottery and many other schemes to get rich quick are so popular. Many want to get rich by focusing attention on their selfish goals without any real concern with the means to reaching the end. Notice what Jesus' description is for this man who makes his possessions an end in themselves. He is a fool. You can select whatever synonym you may want for fool. A fool is a clown, buffoon, dummy, ninny, nincompoop, or a half-wit, but they are all derogatory images no matter which one you select. Jesus calls this man a fool, yet many today might admire and imitate him. Look at the man. He worked hard, saved his money, was industrious, and planned for the future. Why was he a fool? He was a fool because his life was measured only by his possessions. He thought that what he had would make him rich. How sad it is indeed! If we attempt to measure our life only by material means, we will wind up on a dead-end street.

THE DANGER OF WEALTH

An Anxiety Creator

Focusing on our possessions can cause us to overlook certain things in our lives. We can overlook the danger that comes from wealth. Danger? Oh, yes.

A minister asked one of his wealthy church members one time: "Do you know that you are in the most dangerous period of your life?"

"What are you talking about? I have more money than I have ever had," the man observed.

"Oh, I know," the minister said. "And that is the reason why you are in such danger."

Prosperity and excessive good fortune should cause us to be cautious. Why? Because prosperity often creates more anxiety. The more we have the more we want.

A reporter asked Mr. Rockefeller how much money he wanted to control. "Oh, just a little bit more." And that is always the case.

In a recent drama on television a man was parading around in a fancy new suit he had bought. His friend asked him: "When will you get enough of these things?"

"No one ever gets enough of the good life," he responds. We always want more, more, MORE. Many live with the constant anxiety that what they have will slip through their fingers. The more they have the more they want.

The Danger of False Security

There is another danger which arises from thinking that our security can be determined by material things. "If I have enough things — possessions — then I will be secure." But Jesus reminds us that "one's life does not consist in the abundance of possessions (Matthew 12:15). Ease and security can not be based on possessions. The novel by Sloan Wilson, *The Man in the Gray Flannel Suit,* which was later made into a movie, tells the story about a man whose company tried to push him to spend so much time at his job making money for the company that he had no time for his family or himself. The story ends with the man rebelling against the company that wanted to absorb his life completely with material ends. Society all too often pushes its men/women in gray or blue flannel suits to pursue money as though it were an end in itself.

GENEROUS GIVING

Our second text for today gives a word from Paul about using our money in Christ's service. In the Apostle Paul's letter to the Corinthians he offers some brief suggestions on how we can use our possessions in a positive way. In this letter Paul was urging the Corinthians to take up a generous offering for him to take to the Jerusalem church in their time of need. Paul begins by telling his readers that giving is like sowing seeds. Many of you, like I did, probably planted some grass seed this fall. We discover, of course, that if we don't sow enough seed in a certain place on our lawns, we are not going to get a good stand of grass. If we broadcast the seeds too thinly, we will get poor results. Even if we broadcast our seed properly, it will still be difficult to grow in some places. Paul says, "If you sow sparingly, you will reap sparingly." Each of us needs to be a part of those who sow our financial seeds generously. Each of us individually, and as a church, has received blessings from God. Each of us is important in this project. We don't need just a few of us giving generously. The strength of this congregation will be realized in every single individual being a part of a generous team.

THE TIME TO GIVE IS NOW

Paul appeals to the Corinthian church to give now to assist the Jerusalem church because the need is in this present time (2 Corinthians 9:1-9). If they do not help now some time in the future may be too late. We can't assume that we can choose some time in the future to give to support the needs of our church's ministry. This is out time for action. None of us knows how long he or she will live. I have spent too much time in hospitals, walked down too many paths in cemeteries with people who thought that they would have more time to do what they wanted to accomplish in life. None of us knows the length of his or her life. We have to be careful to invest ourselves in something that is more lasting than material things.

I read an anecdote out of the Far West which carries a wonderful lesson. A group of hunters had made their camp for the night. For some reason they were called away from their camp. They had left their campfire unattended with a kettle of water boiling on it.

Seeing the abandoned camp site, an old bear crept out of the woods to see if he could find something to eat. Seeing the kettle with its lid dancing about on top, the bear thought it contained food and promptly seized it. The boiling water in the kettle scalded him badly; but instead of dropping the kettle instantly, he proceeded to hug it tightly. Hugging is one of the chief means of defense for a bear. Of course, the tighter the bear hugged the kettle, the more it burned him. The more the kettle burned him, the tighter the bear hugged it. This vicious circle was, of course, the undoing of the bear.

This illustrates perfectly the way in which many people hug their wealth and property to their bosoms. The refusal to let loose some of it to help others, or support their church, or minister to those less fortunate or use a portion of it in some way to serve Christ, rather than helping them grow spiritually, many may discover that their possessions can lead to their own destruction. When covetousness asserts itself in our lives maybe we should recall the old western story about the "Bear hugs kettle," and think about God instead and how we can use our possessions to glorify God.

THE DANGER OF OVERLOOKING THE NEEDS OF OTHERS

Our investments may also cause us to overlook the needs of other people. The Corinthian church might focus only about their own needs and not care about the Jerusalem church and its struggles. Paul knew they had enough to supply their own needs and called them to give generously to help this struggling church in Jerusalem. What would be their attitude toward the use of their material goods to help another? Would they be satisfied to get more material possessions for themselves or see beyond themselves to help another church in need? Would they decide to find genuine happiness in ease and getting more for themselves rather than sharing out of their surplus to those less fortunate in Jerusalem? He challenges them to give generously and not "sow sparingly" because "God loves a cheerful giver." Paul did not want them to think that their wealth came from their own resources. This would cause them to overlook the importance of God in their lives. They should not think that their material things had been acquired through their own efforts alone. Many overlook the power of God, and the fact that God underlies the foundation of our lives. Our wealth, money, and possessions can sometimes become blinders and keep us from seeing how to use financial means properly. There is always the danger that prosperity can alienate us from God.

Jenny Lind, a famous Swedish soprano, surprised many by turning down a number of concerts she was asked to perform. One of her friends came by when she was sitting on the seashore one day with her Bible open on her lap. Her friend rebuked her for not taking advantage of the tours she had been offered. Miss Lind lifted her Bible from her lap and said: "I found that making vast sums of money was spoiling my taste for this."

Are we going to let our possessions become ends in themselves or will we listen to the words of warning from our Lord about the idolatry of possessions?

THE CHURCH BUILDING AND ETERNAL VALUES

When our congregation was displaced and we met for worship on the seminary campus while our building was being constructed, a young man walked out the chapel door one Sunday morning and asked me an interesting question. He held up our church bulletin, which had the proposed image of our new church sanctuary on the cover. "I want to ask you about this picture," pointing to the artist's sketch on the bulletin cover. "What does this building have to do with the eternal values of God which you spoke about this morning?" It was a good question. What does this building — our sanctuary — which is now built; have to do with eternal values? What does a church building have to teach us about "not laying up for yourselves treasures on earth?" What does this building have to do with religious truths? Everything! This building sits in this community, in our city, as a symbol that sin is real. If sinfulness was not real, we wouldn't need this building. It has been constructed to provide us a place where we are constantly challenged to reach up to the highest standard — to be like God. This church building challenges us to see that our lives are not measured primarily by physical or material things, but spiritual values. This building is symbolic of the presence of God in our lives and community. Its presence calls us to commit ourselves to deeper causes and more spiritual values and material ends. I give my offering not to a building but what this building symbolizes and the spiritual lessons which are taught in and through this building. "Buildings witness. We are their stewards — not solely for the internal purpose of the church," Patricia Farris writes in *Pastor, Person, Healer, Prophet, Pilgrim*, but for all the ways our very buildings proclaim a message of God's inclusive, welcoming, sheltering, and community-creating love."[11] Buildings are often very important indeed.

THE RIGHT ATTITUDE IN GIVING

Paul reminds his readers that they should give with a sense of joy, not grudgingly. The right attitude is not: "Oh, gosh, I have to give some more money to church. When will they quit asking?" We can never give enough to God. We give out of a sense of joy for what God has done for us. God loves a "cheerful giver." Paul says that when we give generously it has an affect on three persons. It will first of all affect the giver. It will affect you and me. Because it gets us outside ourselves. Generous giving takes the spotlight off self-interest and selfishness and enables us to focus on what God can do in and through us. Generosity gives us a whole different sense of values.

Suppose you were told that some awful phenomenon had happened in our world that turned life upside down. You were then informed that the only way you could survive was not by having money to spend but by having books. I picked books because I have a lot of them. If you knew that the only way you could survive today was to have books, would you not want to have a lot of books? You would want to find out what you needed to do to get these books. You would want to transfer and exchange everything else you had for books, if they were essential for survival. If books will make life different, you would give anything you could to acquire them.

This analogy points to the importance of an exchange principle. This may point us to the truth that Jesus was trying to tell us about. Jesus challenges us to invest our lives in certain ways so that

1   Patricia Farris, *Pastor, Parson, Healer, Prophet, Pilgrim* (Nashville: Abingdon Press, 2015), 32.

later it will pay off heavenly benefits. "Lay not up for yourselves treasures on earth where moth and rust doth corrupt, but lay up for yourselves treasures in heaven." How do you do that? You do that by committing everything you have — not just a part of your life — but your total possessions to God. You utilize all you possess in a way that glorifies God. Get out of your self-centeredness and find ways to focus your life upon God.

I heard about a man who told a friend of his about all the land he owned and all the possessions and wealth which he had accumulated. He told his friend, as he pointed North, South, East and West, that he owned all the land as far as he could see. "I can see in the directions where you pointed all that you own," his friend stated. "But what do you have of any value that goes in this direction (as he pointed upward toward heaven)?" What have you done with all of your material possessions to lay something aside that will be eternal? You can't take your money, houses or land with you. Have you utilized your possessions in any way that blesses, or helps other people?

GIVE TO HELP OTHERS

This leads us to our second investment from generous giving. It not only affects us but other people as well, Paul said. When you give generously you help others. You meet needs which they have. Your gracious gifts restore the faith of others in you. Your financial gifts show that you mean what you say when you talk about loving God. You demonstrate your faith by putting your money where your mouth is. I am not convinced that any individual really, genuinely loves God who does not commit his or her money to spiritual causes. I do not know how I can say it any more clearly than that. The Scriptures indicate that when we refuse to commit our money to ways which glorify God, we are blinded to the genuine values of life.

William White gave the city of Emporia fifty acres to be used for a city park as a memorial to his daughter. He gave it under the condition that the park not bear his name. When he gave the deed to the mayor, he said: "This is the last kick in a fistful of dollars I am getting rid of today. I have always tried to teach that there are three kicks in every dollar, one when you make it ... the second kick is when you have it ... The third kick comes when you give it away . . . The big kick is in the last one." Most of us only get two kicks out of money. We miss the last one, because we have never discovered the joy of giving it to help other people.

Give to Glorify God

Finally, Paul says that giving affects God. We give as an expression of our praise for God and as a way to glorify Him. We give out of thanksgiving for God's unspeakable — indescribable — gift through Jesus Christ. "His gift beyond words" as *the New English Bible* translates it. We give so we might glorify God.

We all have demands on our lives, but one of our greatest priorities is to determine how we will use our money. Your church needs your faithful tithe and offerings week-after- week as representation of your devotion to God. We need you to be a part of those who support your church on a regular basis week-by-week and as a faithful participant in this special drive. What are you laying down on earth for your heavenly investments?

A number of years ago Helen Hayes was traveling by train, and a passenger approached her, introduced herself, and told her about an actor friend on the train who was dying. She asked if Miss Hayes could come by and speak to her friend, who had heard that Miss Hayes was on the train and wanted to meet her. Miss Hayes indicated that she would be happy to come by. Miss Hayes stopped by this woman's private compartment and talked with her. While they were talking, this woman asked her nurse if she would bring her box of jewels to her so she could show her jewels to Miss Hayes. Miss Hayes watched this woman who was dying as she opened her box of jewels and took out one piece after another and described how and when she got it. She listened attentively to the dying woman, but walked away thinking how pathetic this situation was. Here was a woman, who was dying, and all she could think or talk about was the contents of her box of jewels and what they meant to her. She had no friends. No one was there, except a nurse, while she was dying. She had spent her life hoarding instead of giving.

There are a lot of things that money cannot buy. The most important choice we make in life is our relationship with God and our eternal salvation. We can't take our possessions with us. I choose to invest my money, time, and effort in something that will reap eternal rewards. I challenge you to do the same.

O God of gracious giving, You have loved us beyond our imagination and blessed us beyond what we deserve. May we learn to give lovingly, generously, and cheerfully. Through Christ who has given His all for us, we pray. Amen.

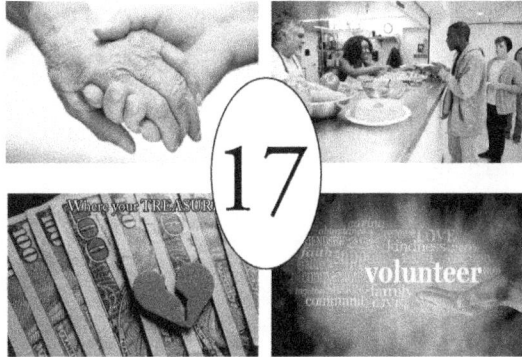

"STEWARDSHIP OF THE EARTH: LIVING AT PEACE WITH THE ENVIRONMENT"

Psalm 19:1-5; Romans 8:19-22; Revelation 21:1, 22:1-2

What does all this discussion about ecology; the environment and pollution have to do with the church, Christians and the Bible? It's an interesting question. Questions sometimes can help us get to the truth.

Consider a fable. There was a little city dog, well, not so little, a big city dog named Scotty. He decided to go visit his farm dog friends. Upon arriving at the farm, he told them that he was the toughest dog that could be found anyplace and he would take any of them on to show how tough he was. "Well," they said, "we know you are probably a tough dog. We have got two critters here that we have not been able to take care of. If you can beat them, we know that you are indeed a tough dog. The first one is black and has a little white stripe down its back. We'd like for you to take care of him. Do you have any questions?" The city dog responded, "No questions, I'll take care of him." So he went rushing in and in a few moments they picked him up and dragged him back. And he says, "He never laid a glove on me. He threw tear gas at me." They said, "Well we have another creature we want you to fight." Scotty looked at him. "Do you have any questions?" they asked. "No questions, he doesn't look too tough," Scotty replied.

Scotty rushed in to meet the new creature. In a few moments the dogs dragged him back. As they were pulling the quills from him, Scotty said, "He didn't lay a glove on me. He threw knives at me. Now that I know how you country dogs fight, I'll go in and take care of these two critters." So he covered his nose with one paw to protect him from the odor, and he covered his eyes with the other paw to protect him from the knives, and he rushed in to fight the two animals. Not being able to see or smell; he was soundly defeated. Now the moral of this story is: it is better to ask a few questions, than to have all the answers.

IS THE CHURCH RESPONSIBLE FOR THE ENVIRONMENTAL CRISIS?

We need to ask some questions about the whole problem with the environment, pollution and ecology. The first question is this — do churches and Christians have any responsibility for the crises in which we find ourselves today? There are some scientists who are saying, "Oh yes, Churches and Christians are largely responsible for this crisis." Lynn White and other scientists are expounding that attitude. They point to the passage in Genesis which says, "Man is supposed to subdue the earth" and note that we have subdued it to the point of devastation. These scientists believe that Christians are responsible because of the philosophy and theology taken from Genesis, of subduing the earth. Are we responsible? Well, yes and no.

THE HEBREW CONCEPT OF NATURE

The Greeks had the notion that the human body and nature itself were evil. There was nothing inside of man and woman that was pure or good but the soul. The Hebrews did not have that attitude toward life. The body was not seen as corrupt but good. They saw humankind as being one with God and was supposed to be linked with others and also to creation itself. In fact, when you read the scriptures you discover that the Hebrews had a high concept of nature. Nature seemed almost alive itself. Nature is alive with God's creation. The marvelous passage from Psalms 19 declares that the heavens and the earth disclose God to us. The Hebrews did not see creation as evil in itself but as good and as a part of God's wonderful creation. A special covenant had been made with them by the great God of the universe. William Blake, the poet, expressed the truth this way:

> To see a world in a grain of sand
> And a heaven in wild flowers.
> Hold infinity in the palm of your hand and eternity in an hour.

NATURE REVEALS GOD

In the biblical perspective of creation human beings are able to look at the wonder of creation and it should disclose God to us. The natural world is not God, but the Creator is revealed through it. An emperor, years ago in a Chinese country asked an artist to paint him a picture of a rooster. "I will do it," the artist replied, "but it will take me a long time." After several years had passed, the emperor asked the artist if he had finished the painting. "No, not yet," he responded, "I can see a little of the external part of the rooster." Ten years passed and the artist finally brought the emperor his painting of a rooster. As the emperor looked at it, he saw revealed within that rooster, not just a bird, but it seemed infinity itself, creation itself, was disclosed in the beauty, mystery and marvel of that painting. When we have eyes "to see," we should be able to see in a rooster, a bird, an animal or a flower, or whatever, something of the awesome mystery of God in his wonderful creation.

UNFULFILLED CREATION

Something, however, has gone wrong with God's creation. Sin is a part of creation and we are not quite able to understand what happened in God's good world. Two men were fishing one day and one of them observed: "I don't understand. What is the purpose of fish? A big fish eats a small fish and a bigger fish eats that fish. Was that fish just created to be eaten by the bigger fish?" Life sometimes doesn't seem fair, does it? One of the things the scriptures tell us is that creation is good, but it is not perfect. Paul tells us in the eighth chapter of Romans that creation is in travail and is moving toward being fulfilled. Creation itself will be redeemed by God. One day there will be a new heaven and a new earth. Creation itself will fully be redeemed by God's glorious grace. Creation is moving toward fulfilling what it was created to be. Humankind has the responsibility of living in harmony with and not in opposition to nature. In his interpretation of the *Book of Revelation*, Mitchell Reddish depicts "the River of Life" in the description of "the New Heaven and the New Earth" and the "New Jerusalem" as having "life-giving properties, nourishing the trees on its banks and turning the life-less, foul waters of the Dead Sea into waters teeming with fish."[1] But that image is in the vision of a fulfilled creation. We are not there yet.

THE PRODIGAL WAY OF HUMANITY

What then is the nature of our responsibility? Humankind has been like the prodigal son. We have taken all the blessings God has given us and we have wasted them in riotous living, sometimes in excessive living. We have received the bounty of God's creation and we have exploited and sometimes ruined it. I wish I could stand in this pulpit today and tell you that all of our rivers and streams are pure, and that our air is pure, and the water we drink is fine. But no person can truthfully tell you that today. Many of the trees on the mountaintops of North Carolina are dying because of pollution. It is a serious problem. Just a few years ago, we couldn't eat oysters taken from our own coast in Virginia because of the refuse and waste that had been dumped into our waters and they were so impure. Even the ocean itself was polluted. We still have factories that spew impurities into our water and into our air today.

1   Mitchell G. Reddish, *Revelation: Smyth & Helwys Commentary* (Macon, GA: Smyth & Helwys Publishing Co., 2001), 419.

Did you know that there are some cities where the air is so thick with pollution that when you breathe the air it is the equivalent of smoking thirty-eight cigarettes a day? I am convinced that one of the reasons we have such a rise in cancer is because the water we drink and the air we breathe and the foods we eat are polluted. Much of life is filled with the problems of living with pollution. You and I, as citizens, have to work hard to overcome these abuses of our land, air and water.

A few years ago, a farmer named Robert Musick who raised goats in the Pipal Mountains of Arizona discovered that after herbicides were sprayed on the trees in the Tonto National Forest that 60 percent of his kid goats were either born dead or deformed. A peach grower nearby, who had his peach crop there for a quarter of a century, found that after the herbicides had been sprayed, his peaches shriveled up and were black and as hard as rocks. Now, we know we have to have some pesticides. But we human beings have got to understand and work to find pesticides that work with our environment, and do not harm us, our children, or our crops, land, air and water. We have a serious responsibility to see what we can do to avoid being prodigals with our universe.

Suppose someone told you that you have a bank account with enough money in that account to take care of you all your life, if you don't overspend. If you spend carefully and wisely, you will always have enough in your account. You don't know the exact amount in your account and you are never going to be told that. But you do know that if you just spend wisely you will always have enough. You would be very careful wouldn't you?

Our environment is that way. We can't just keep on abusing, and destroying rainforests and other parts of the natural world without bringing devastation upon ourselves and our world. Some view environmentalists as "cocoons" and pretend that we do not have a serious problem. But, it is serious! Denying global warming and pretending climate change is not happening is like sticking our head in the sand. We have to realize that our children and grandchildren and others may not be able to live in our world unless we take care of it. *National Geographic* devoted the September 2004 issue to "Global Warming" and warned that "the climate is changing at an unnerving pace. Glaciers are retreating, ice shelves are fracturing, sea level is rising, permafrost is melting."[1] The April 3, 2006 issue of *Time* magazine was entitled "Special Report Global Warming," and warned that "climate change isn't some vague future problem — it's already damaging the planet at an alarming pace."[2] George Philander, professor of geosciences at Princeton, declares that there are many aspects of global warning that are still only dimly understood by scientists. He acknowledges that humanity is disturbing the natural cycles which we really do not understand very well. It's like; he projects, being in "a ship in the fog in treacherous waters.... We should be doing something, not because we know what's going to happen, but because we don't know what's going to happen."[3]

CARETAKERS OF OUR PLANET

As Christian people we have a responsibility. What is that responsibility? Our responsibility is to be stewards and caretakers of God's universe. The Genesis story doesn't tell us that we are to devour the earth or we can do anything we want with nature. God placed Adam and Eve in the Garden to take care of it. They were to be caretakers and "to tend the earth." We are to work with nature and learn how to live in harmony with creation. All of God's creation is our home. And it is a beautiful home. We have got to learn how to live in harmony with God's creation and to do the very best thing we can to care for it and make it a place that is beautiful and productive. One of our responsibilities as Christians is to do those things which can make this earth the very best place where we can live. It is our home-our only home-and we have to take care of it by conserving its resources and productivity.

---

1   Daniel Glick, "The Big Thaw," *National Geographic* (September 2004), 13.
2   *Time*, (April 3, 2006), front cover.
3   Eileen Flanagan, "Temperature Rising," *The Christian Century* (August 21, 2013), 26.

Pope Francis's encyclical, *Laudato Si'*, released on June 19, 2015 made a passionate call "to every person living on the planet" to respond to the reality of climate change as "one of the principal challenges facing humanity in our day." He rebuffed the arguments of climate skeptics and challenged the interpretation of those who used the book of Genesis wording that is frequently quoted to denote man's "dominion" over the Earth, and hence exploitation of its resources for our selfish needs. Pope Francis is unequivocal in the encyclical that "this is not a correct interpretation of the Bible as understood by the church." He declared that we must respect the laws of nature and protect the Earth for future generations. Humans are part of nature, not its overlords, he affirms, and caring for ourselves and for nature is inseparable in caring for our common home.[1] Whether we are Catholics or Protestants or of no religious tradition, his argument strikes home. In February of 2006 eighty-six Christian leaders, who were so vitally concerned about climate change, formed what was called the "Evangelical Climate Initiative" and demanded that Congress regulate greenhouse gases.[2] In his book, *Our Endangered Values: America's Moral Crisis,* former President, Jimmy Carter, in addressing the major threats to the environment declared boldly: "Our proper stewardship of God's world is a personal and political moral commitment."[3]

The scientist, Pierre Teilhard de Chardin has reminded us that, "The Age of Nations is past. The task before us now, if we will not perish, is to build the earth." We are all responsible for our planet. We can't pass the responsibility to others.

---

1 www.theguardian.com *"Exegesis of Pope Francis's encyclical call for action on climate change."*
   To read the encyclical see: *http://w2.vatican.va/content/francesco/en/ encyclical/documents/papafrancesco_20150524_enciclica-laudato-si.html.*

2 Jeffrey Kluger, "By Any Measure, Earth Is at the Tipping Point," *Time* (April 3, 2006), 35.

3 Jimmy Carter, *Our Endangered Values: America's Moral Crisis* (New York: Simon & Schuster, 2005), 177.

As Robert Louis Stevenson was walking down the street one day, he saw a man beating his dog, unmercifully. Stevenson cried out to the man, "Don't do that to your dog."

"It's my dog," the man replied, "I can do whatever I want to it."

Stevenson said, "No, it's God's dog."

The entire universe is God's. You and I are responsible for our actions toward all of creation. Nobody can say he or she can do anything one wants to our planet, or dump anything into our streams, or spew anything into the air. You and I have a responsibility as Christian persons to seek to do our part in trying to make this a better place to live.

Francis of Assisi (1182-1226) in his *The Canticle of Brother Sun* has voiced our prayer for the environment:

O most high, almighty, good Lord God,
to you belong praise, glory, honor, and all blessing.

Praised be my Lord God with all his
creatures and specially our brother the sun,
who brings us the day and who brings us light;
fair is he and shines with a very great splendor.
O Lord, he shows us you.

Praised be my Lord for our sister the moon,
and for the stars,
which he has set clear and lovely in the heavens.

Praised be my Lord for our brother the wind,
and for the air and cloud, calms,
and all weather by which you uphold life in all creatures.

Praised be my Lord for our brother fire,
through whom you give us light in the darkness;
and he is bright and pleasant and very strong.
Praised be my Lord for our mother the earth,

who sustains us and keep us and brings forth diverse fruits
and flowers of many colors, and grass.

Praised be my Lord for all those
who pardon one another for his love's sake,
and who endure weakness and tribulation.
Blessed are they who peaceably shall endure.

Praised be my Lord for our sister the death of the body,
from which no man escapes.
Blessed are those who are found walking
by your most holy will.
Praise and bless the Lord; and give thanks to him;
and serve him with great humility.
Amen.[1]

SOME PRACTICAL SUGGESTIONS

What can we do? Let me offer some simple, practical suggestions.

First. Be informed. Be aware that we still have a serious pollution problem in our world. Acknowledge that our leading world
scientists have all attested to global warming and the reality of climate change. They have all called the world to work for a solution
to the world-wide problem before it is too late. To deny this reality
is foolish and dangerous.

Second. Teach our children. Teach them to be responsible citizens in our world. They can do simple things like learning how to
take care of garbage and litter by putting these things in their proper place. In a community where I once lived they did away with
our recycling plastic and newspaper recycling centers. That is just
absolutely unbelievable to me. We need to get behind our officials
and say to them, "We need to have recycling introduced again."

---

1 "The Canticle of Brother Sun," *Late Medieval Mysticism, The Library of Christian Classics*, vol. XIII, edited by Ray C, Petry (Philadelphia: The Westminster Press, 1957), 124-125.

We need to recycle our newspapers, plastic, glass and aluminum. There is no reason why this cannot be done. There are people who will collect these items and use them effectively. I am glad to live in a community that collects our recycled items routinely now. We as citizens need to express our concern about these things and teach our children the proper way to care for our environment.

I remember a few years ago, I went on a trip to Canada with some friends. There was a person in our group who was a heavy smoker. After he got out of the car in Canada, he dumped his ashtray on the asphalt at the service station. The man at the service station didn't say a word to him. Instead, he came down with a little broom and swept the ashtray litter into a container. He then discarded it in a trash can nearby. My friend realized what he had done and apologized.

That is so like us. Without thinking we pitch out a piece of paper, or throw a paper cup on the ground. We forget the thousands of dollars it costs for somebody to pick it up. We need to educate our children and ourselves in how to be more responsible for caring for our planet.

Third. We need, on occasion, to write our senators, congressmen, mayor and other governmental leaders to let them know that we want everything that can be done in research and practical laws that will make this a better place to live. We need to put pressure on government and industry to do what is right and work on the global warming problem.

Fourth. We as a worshiping community should gather and celebrate God's creation. We need to learn how to live better in harmony with our universe. God has given us a beautiful world. Why would we want to do anything that is going to make it less than beautiful? Through the raising of our crops, trees, fruit, animals and everything that we do we want to learn how to live in harmony with nature. Let us love and protect the environment. That seems to me to be a vital part of our responsibility as stewards of God's earth. Let us continue to work to that end.

The sermon today has no conclusion. You see; you and I must conclude it. We will conclude it by assuming our responsibility to be good citizens and good caretakers and stewards of God's environment. Let's learn to live in peace with God's creation. God has given us a good world. Let's keep it good.

O Gracious God we thank You for Your creation. Forgive us when we have spoiled it. Forgive us when we have not raised our voices when we have seen what others have done harm to it. Give us the courage to be those individuals that will seek to help make our planet a better place to live, for ourselves, our children, grandchildren and generations to come. We pray in the name of the One who is the Prince of Peace, Jesus Christ, our Lord. Amen.

ALSO FROM ENERGION PUBLICATIONS

Bill Tuck always seems to know how to weave the biblical, inspirational, personal, and practical together for maximum impact.

Ron Higdon
Retired pastor, teacher, and author

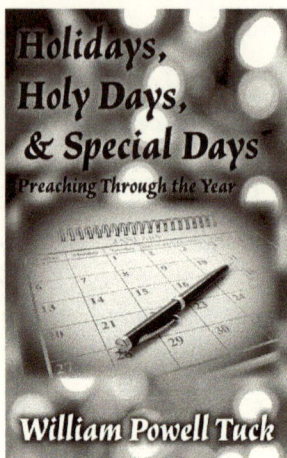

Holidays, Holy Days, & Special Days
Preaching Through the Year

William Powell Tuck

ALSO BY WILLIAM POWELL TUCK

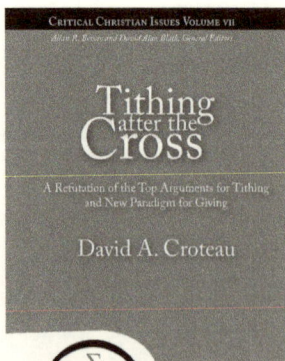

CRITICAL CHRISTIAN ISSUES VOLUME VII

Tithing after the Cross

A Refutation of the Top Arguments for Tithing and New Paradigm for Giving

David A. Croteau

AREOPAGUS
CRITICAL CHRISTIAN ISSUES

Here is essential reading for the Christian who wants to be biblically obedient!

Craig L. Blomberg, Ph.D.
Denver Seminary, Denver, CO

MORE FROM ENERGION PUBLICATIONS

Personal Study

Finding My Way in Christianity	Herold Weiss	$16.99
Holy Smoke! Unholy Fire	Bob McKibben	$14.99
The Jesus Paradigm	David Alan Black	$17.99
When People Speak for God	Henry Neufeld	$17.99
The Sacred Journey	Chris Surber	$11.99

Christian Living

Faith in the Public Square	Robert D. Cornwall	$16.99
Grief: Finding the Candle of Light	Jody Neufeld	$8.99
Crossing the Street	Robert LaRochelle	$16.99

Bible Study

Learning and Living Scripture	Lentz/Neufeld	$12.99
From Inspiration to Understanding	Edward W. H. Vick	$24.99
Luke: A Participatory Study Guide	Geoffrey Lentz	$8.99
Philippians: A Participatory Study Guide	Bruce Epperly	$9.99
Ephesians: A Participatory Study Guide	Robert D. Cornwall	$9.99

Theology

Creation in Scripture	Herold Weiss	$12.99
Creation: the Christian Doctrine	Edward W. H. Vick	$12.99
The Politics of Witness	Allan R. Bevere	$9.99
Ultimate Allegiance	Robert D. Cornwall	$9.99
History and Christian Faith	Edward W. H. Vick	$9.99
The Church Under the Cross	William Powell Tuck	$11.99
The Journey to the Undiscovered Country	William Powell Tuck	$9.99
Eschatology: A Participatory Study Guide	Edward W. H. Vick	$9.99

Ministry

Clergy Table Talk	Kent Ira Groff	$9.99
Out of This World	Darren McClellan	$24.99

Generous Quantity Discounts Available
Dealer Inquiries Welcome
Energion Publications — P.O. Box 841
Gonzalez, FL_ 32560
Website: http://energionpubs.com
Phone: (850) 525-3916

www.ingramcontent.com/pod-product-compliance
Lightning Source LLC
Chambersburg PA
CBHW030925090426
42737CB00007B/326